HUMOROUS MONOLOGUES
FOR TEEN-AGERS

HUMOROUS

MONOLOGUES / FOR

TEEN-AGERS

A COLLECTION OF ROYALTY-FREE
DRAMATIC SKETCHES FOR YOUNG PEOPLE

By Robert Fontaine

Publishers   PLAYS, INC.   *Boston*

Library of Congress Catalog Card Number: 63-15361

ISBN: 08238-0125-X

MANUFACTURED IN THE UNITED STATES OF AMERICA

CONTENTS

HUMOROUS MONOLOGUES
FOR TEEN-AGERS

1 HOW TO WRITE FOR THE MOVIES

(The scene is the office of Glamor Movie Productions. SAM HOSER *is sitting at his desk, talking on the telephone.)*

Hello. Glamor Movie Productions, Inc. Who? Tab Wagner? No. He's on the set making *Remember Mother's Pickles.* They're shooting the deathbed scene where the drummer boy is dying at Gettysburg and he asks for one more jar of his mother's pickles. O.K. *(Hangs up. Turns to visitor.)*

Sit down, Mr. Gilmore. I'm proud and pleased to have you working with Glamor Productions. Not many eminent novelists, Nobel Prize winners and world-renowned authors write for us. We bought your novel, *New England Dream,* because what we are always looking for is a picture that is sweet, clean, tender and a best seller.

This book of yours, Mr. Gilmore, embodies the spirit of poetry and beauty. It is light and gentle, and yet it leaves you knowing more about your own heart and about the world.

Now, Mr. Gilmore, you realize, being an educated man, that a motion picture is not a book. Certain small changes of a technical nature must be made. . . . What? Oh, very minor changes indeed. . . .

What's that? Oh, no. I have the greatest respect for literary art. That is one thing I shall never tamper with. But, there are certain minor matters I must discuss. (*Telephone rings. He answers.*)

Hello. Sam Hoser here, executive producer. What? No. I won't need a hundred. Eighty-five elephants will be enough. And a few crocodiles. Huh? Oh, yes, an Egyptian barge. Right. Check. (*Hangs up. To Gilmore*)

Those are *your* elephants, my boy. Not everybody gets eighty-five elephants for his picture, *and* several crocodiles. We are going, as a matter of fact, to reconstruct the whole Nile River near Las Vegas, but I'm ahead of myself. (*Listens thoughtfully*)

What, Mr. Gilmore? No elephants in your book? I know that, Mr. Gilmore. But we have to think *big*. Your book needs elephants. Just be patient and I'll explain. What we want to do is express in pictures what we know was in the back of your mind but you couldn't put into words.

Now, one minor change is that the hero in the picture will have to be a girl—a heroine, that is. Something like Cleopatra. Eh? Yes, well, Cleopatra won't *be* in New England. That's another minor change we have to make. We're shifting the locale from New England in the 1890's to Egypt in the time of the Pharaohs. (*Pause*)

This will *not* basically change what you have to say, Mr. Gilmore. Your story is about a young boy, afraid of love, who falls for this older schoolteacher who brings him tenderness and strength. All very touching. No one likes New England more than I do. But Egypt is more colorful. Elephants. Crocodiles. The boy becomes a young queen who finds herself surrounded by enemy armies. A sort of Egyptian Joan of Arc with a figure like Bardot. I have just the girl. . . .

Don't interrupt me, Mr. Gilmore, until you have heard me out. Fair is fair. And I suggest you stop chewing on your hat. The color may run.

Now, we have two boys working on a theme song— *My Heart With Love Is Overflowing Like the Nile*— something like that. Another one is called: *The Sphinx Knows About Our Love*. Oh, I guess I didn't mention that we are turning this into a musical drama in glorious color. Your schoolteacher becomes a rival queen. Instead of being a sad New Englander, she becomes a gay Egyptian. She takes baths in wine and rose petals and has people beheaded all the time. A real person you can identify yourself with. Someone to root *against*.

Can I get you some water, Mr. Gilmore? You look pale. No? Fine. Now, a Roman soldier falls for this Egyptian— are you listening, Mr. Gilmore? It's *your* book. This Roman soldier is the counterpart of the sad little janitor in your book. . . . Eh? I'm afraid, Mr. Gilmore, sad little janitors are not much in demand by the public. Handsome Roman soldiers *are*.

Be patient, Mr. Gilmore. I've put a lot of money and thought into this. The Roman soldier falls in love with the bad queen, see? Everybody wants him to fall for the good queen. The bad queen taunts him and haunts him —good line for a song there—and he is just about beat, wandering across the desert, having hallucinations about Rome. This gives us a chance to bring in the dream sequence. Remember in your book . . . you *do* remember your book, Mr. Gilmore? Good. Sit up, please. I keep thinking you're sick. Your dream sequence had the boy dreaming of when he was a child dancing alone in the meadows of Lexington or Concord or wherever it was. . . . What? Oh, yes, that's another book. Marblehead. Yes. Well, we have improved that scene vastly. In the dream of the Roman soldier instead of the dance we have him see Rome again . . . a great orgy. For *this*—now get this—for this we are training eighty-five elephants to do a cha-cha! You see, it's a dream, so we can do anything. Harry Rudolph has come up with a great comic song, *Can You Teach an Elephant to Cha-Cha.*

Well, the good queen happens to be on a crocodile hunt—this corresponds to your county fair—and she comes across the Roman soldier and they fall in love instantly, marry, and he becomes her consort amid a splendor you would hardly believe, all in glorious color, with music and an elephant ballet.

Mr. Gilmore, *please,* you seem upset. Why are you upset? All we have done is bring to the *front* what was in the back of your mind when you wrote your brilliant book. We have *not* touched the *essence* of it . . .

Mr. Gilmore, I beg you—don't cry. I hate to see a grown man cry. And stop tearing your hat to shreds. I'll have the studio nurse come in and look at you. . . . (*Rushes out*)

THE END

2 DUTCH TREAT

(This monologue finds a mature woman, AMY FEATHERS, who has just had lunch with several of her girl friends, called upon to split up the check and collect from the others. She has her troubles.)

I can't help it, Ethel; they don't give separate checks here at the Cafe Royal. Now, Ethel, calling it an exclusive dump isn't going to help. They have a single check for each party so that the waiter is kept . . . well, I don't know . . . I guess he's kept distinguished from the others. I don't *know*, Ethel. I can't see that it matters in the least.

What's that, Lois? . . . Ask the waiter again? All right. Oh, garçon! Waiter! Yoo-hoo, number 17! Sev-unn-*tee*-un! Ah, here you are. Could you go back and make out separate checks for us? Pardon? Well, after our canasta game we like to eat out, but it would be awkward if one person paid the check because—it would. You despise canasta? I'm sorry. But I don't see what it has to do with the serious matter of getting the check straightened out.

Oh, I see. You haven't the slightest idea who had what.
. . . We changed our minds so many times that you got
confused? . . . The who? Oh, the chef had to eat two
orders of French fries himself or waste them. Well, that's
what he's there for. All right, all right.

What's that, Anne? Howard Johnson's the next time?
Anne, dear, that helps us not one whit right now. (*Sighs*)
I have no idea what a whit is, Lois. I think it's something
on the boiled dinner.

What, Ethel? Please don't all talk at once. . . . Split
it right down the middle? That only gives us two checks.
Split it in quarters, evenly? Well, maybe. . . .

Beg pardon, Lois? (*Listens*) Uh-huh, uh-huh, I know,
I know. Yes. You're on a diet and you didn't eat half as
much as the rest. True, but you had the lobster sauté, and
that's more expensive than the boiled dinner.

I'm *trying* to listen to Anne. What? Lois had an extra
dessert? I don't think it was extra. It *cost* ten cents extra
because of the whipped cream. I see.

I know, waiter. Just be patient. You're a waiter, so wait.
What, Lois? No. You see, the bill just says ten dollars plus
five per cent old age tax. That's ten dollars and fifty cents.
It doesn't say what, dear. You may be against the old age
tax, Anne, but don't forget we may be old ourselves some
day and be very glad of assistance. What's that, waiter?
. . . We'll be old just trying to get the tab settled? Well,
well, a comical waiter. Nothing like a comical waiter to
cheer us up. Look, garçon . . . what? Antonio? All right.
Regard, Antonio, the bill. Now . . .

Anne, will you please be quiet. We've been friends for
years. I'm taking tranquillizers *now* to calm me down
and something else to pep me up and snakeroot to keep

me in the middle and codeine or something to ease the pain of being in the middle and . . .

Very well, girls, let's start all over. Now, Antonio, rack your brains, if possible. Lois had the turtle soup . . . the lobster sauté . . . hold the French fries . . . June peas. . . . What, Lois? You had no June peas? The waiter says you had. All right, they're free anyway. They come with the lobster. Well, *I* didn't eat them. They come— there, you see, the waiter just found one on the floor. That proves it! How much is all that? . . . What, Antonio? She had a double order of chocolate fudge sundae with extra walnuts? Some diet, Lois. All right, so you didn't have the regular dinner. It was à la carte. That's what, Antonio? Three dollars even.

I heard you, Lois. I understand. You sent back the French fries. There is no refund. They come with the lobster. Whether the chef ate them or not, there is no refund.

Now, Ethel had the blue plate special, right, Antonio? Ethel is the one with the glasses and the feathers . . . in her hat. *I* wouldn't call her the chubby one, but you're entitled to your opinion. Although the statement certainly will not help your cause. She did? All right. The blue plate was corned beef, cabbage, rolls, tomato juice and mince pie. Two dollars. Wait a minute. I've got to write this down. (*Writes in notebook, then looks up quickly*)

What about the mince pie, Ethel? You gave it to Anne because it came with the dinner. But Anne says she gave *you* her Indian pudding that came with her dinner. Which is worth more, Antonio? Antonio, you are not listening. If you think *you* have a headache what do you think *I* have?

What's this for, Ethel? Twenty cents toward the tip?
Wait, Anne . . . all right, you can make change for *your*
tip later. It's ten per cent, maybe, but then there's the
five per cent old age assistance tax on meals in this state.
Well, it wouldn't make much sense to go to another state.
They probably have a dog tax on meals there, or a cover
charge or something. In New Hampshire I think they
used to have a fish tax to restock the trout streams. . . .

Now, Anne had a dessert worth five cents more. I don't
see how it could be worth more if they both came *with*
the dinner. . . . Oh, one dinner was worth more. Ethel
. . . Lois . . . please don't get the change mixed up—
wait until we're all done, and we'll establish a ratio for
the tip. Isn't that best, waiter? You couldn't care less? I
don't call that cooperation.

Now, Anne had the regular dinner: two pork chops and
all that, with the mushed grits, chopped chicken livers,
onion soup. . . . What was that, Antonio? The onion
soup is thirty-five cents? But she had it on the dinner.
Anne, I *beg* you, don't flare up. Everything will be straightened out. This is worse than the United Nations trying
to admit another country. What, Antonio? Much worse?

You see, Anne, dear, it says "Choice of soup or appe-
tizer." Not both. I see. Can't you make a small concession
here, Antonio? It might get confusing. Most places, my
friend claims, give you both on the regular dinner. (*Listens*)

See the owner? Where is he? . . . In Florida? That's a
help. Well, we all know what *I* had. I had the cherry-
stones . . . fifty cents extra . . . the chicken with wild
rice . . . and then the strawberry parfait.

What, waiter? I know you have a headache and I know

you have other customers. It'll all be over in a minute. This, too, shall pass, as they say. Let's see . . . two and two is four . . . eight and eight is fifteen and one to carry . . . two, eleven . . . Hmm. I get $11.55. No you don't, Antonio. I probably added it wrong. Ten dollars plus fifty cents tax is right. I know there was an extra coffee. You don't charge for extra coffee, do you? I don't know who had the extra coffee. Most places— (*Pause*) I *know* you don't get coffee for nothing. But there is a vast surplus in Brazil, and . . .

Please, Anne . . . Ethel . . . Lois . . . we'll have it in a minute. Now, Antonio, shall we be calm and mature and grown-up and just go all over this once more?

Anne had the lobster sauté which is worth . . . Antonio! *Antonio!* Don't tear it up, Antonio. You don't need . . . (*Long pause as she looks, puzzled, around the table at the others. Then she smiles vaguely.*)

Well, wasn't that nice of him. He just tore up the check and said forget it. (*Pause*) What, dear? Oh, I didn't think he was *screaming* as he ran off—I thought he was singing.

Well, anyway, it does clear everything up. If I'd known it was going to come out this way I'd have eaten the T-bone steak. What, Lois? A tip? Yes, of course. He certainly deserves a tip. Well, let's figure it out. Anne had the regular dinner plus thirty-five cents extra soup, that's . . . What? You won't tip on the extra soup? It's only three and a half cents. All right. Why don't we go home and all calm down and then *mail* it to him? Agreed? Motion carried. (*Exits*)

THE END

3 | FATHERS, DEAR FATHERS . . .

(This monologue is intended for a young man, although it can be delivered by anyone, with the change of a few words. Props are not necessary, but a cigar, pipe, newspaper, football and easy chair can all be used by those who have them available.)

A normal fellow who likes to call on girls or take them on dates is in a tough position these days. You know why? Fathers! There are a lot of different kinds of fathers but they all spell trouble and headaches.

Often a fellow would just rather stay home and study or watch TV than go see a girl, because he knows for sure he is going to run across her father. When a father sees a fellow come to take out his daughter, something happens to that father.

I don't mean that all fathers of girls are mean, or suspicious. Some of them are real palsy-walsy . . . friendly until it's sickening. All of them are a problem, though.

You take the cool type with narrow eyes and a big fat cigar. This father is *always* all dressed up, sometimes even with a vest. His collar is dead white and not a wrinkle. He

wears cuff links an inch square. His shoes shine like dia-
monds. He has this cigar in his hand and he never lights
it. He just wiggles his fingers around it. Once in a while
he smells it, I guess to see if it's gone stale.

Either he doesn't remember when he was a boy and
liked a girl, or he remembers it *too well.* You can hardly
get past the door with this loving daddy-o. He looks as if he
has a sword in his hand, and you think you're standing
on a trap door that's going to spring you down into the
dungeon any second. (*He begins to imitate the father.*)

"What do you want?" he says. "Marge? She know you're
coming? What's your name? George? George what? George
Simpson. Which Simpsons are those? Eh? The *plain*
Simpsons? Don't be frivolous, young man. This is a serious matter. Your father does what? I see. He's a banker?
How big is this bank? Three branches? Well, I never heard
of them. Was your mother a Tasswell? I thought so. The
Virginia Tasswells? You don't know? You don't know
your own mother's lineage? Hmn. (*Pause*) What are you
so jittery about? You concealing something? Yes, Marge
is in. We'll get to her in a moment. (*Glares, narrows eyes
and then raises head sternly*) Before you come in, young
man, I want you to know that I do not stand for any fool-
ishness. One false move and out you go. You understand?
You're going to toe the mark, young fellow, if you want
to be friendly with my daughter. I strongly disapprove of
playing any hot jazz records or using the living room to do
any of these crazy twists and rock and rolls. While sitting
on the divan you will maintain a discreet distance from
Marge. At eleven o'clock you and Marge will be served
hot cocoa and crackers. At eleven-fifteen you will leave.
Is that understood? Have I your solemn promise to abide

by my rules? Good. What? *What?* Oh, you don't *want* to come in? You're just bringing back her overshoes she left in school. . . ." (*The boy chuckles and resumes his own voice.*)

Then there's the dad who is almost the opposite. He welcomes you with open arms, real palsy-walsy. There are usually a couple of girls in his family and no boys. Man, is he glad to have someone who doesn't nag him!

Trouble is, he hardly gives you a chance to be with the girl you're calling on. He's got to take you to the game room and show you his guns. The fact that guns scare the dickens out of you only makes him turn to the six or seven buzz saws he has around. They scare you just as much. He wants to be a real buddy, and while you're going crazy wondering what the girl is doing, waiting for you, he gives you a real man-to-man pitch. (*Imitates the father*)

"Wanna tell you something, son. Start off by putting your foot down. Be a man's man. Get with it on flying, fishing, deer-hunting, poker, mountain climbing and real he-man sports. Don't let the women push you around. Understand? This is man to man. Off the record, see? I feel like a father to the boys who come around here. I have to warn each and every one of you that today you have to stand up to the women. Show them who wears the pants in the family. Never forget the time I threw a pair of my trousers at my wife and said, 'Try these on!' She said, 'They don't fit me.' I said, '*Never forget that,* Emma!'

"You look like a serious fellow, and I know you're keen about my daughter. I won't say anything bad about Marge, except she takes after her mother and if you let her she'll start talking and never shut up. Yak, yak, yak about clothes, about the neighbors, about clothes, about perfume, about clothes and about clothes. What you have to do is be firm and simply tell her to shut up. Nicely. You know what I mean, son? I mean if you want to go have a soda don't let anybody talk you into going to see an expensive movie. Be strong. While you can. Another thing, son . . . (*Stops and listens. Finally shouts*) What's that, dear? The dishes? I forgot to dry them and put them away? Yes, I guess I did. Be right up, my love." (*Boy returns to own voice.*)

This guy has all the answers, but it's too late to do him any good. Then there's a third guy. He really gets on your nerves. This papa acts as if he's indifferent and casual . . . you know, nonchalant. He slumps in his chair with a magazine and just grunts when you come in and sit down on the divan with your girl. (*He sits in chair with paper or magazine to demonstrate. He looks out from behind magazine and grunts, then sits up and speaks.*)

You're supposed to act as if he's not there, but how can you sit around with a girl who makes you feel real swoony when this papa sits there listening behind his magazine? Suppose you start talking about how much you like this girl, and you think her eyes are about as blue as they can get eyes to be these days, and her lips are about as red as red comes, and her voice is about as sweet as voices can possibly be outside of nightingales.

This hidden character in the chair (*Leans back in chair behind magazine*) is going to let out some kind of a bored groan or a wild cough, as if he were ready to leave the premises under conditions where everybody would be glad he remembered to make a will. (*He imitates the father, letting out a loud combined cough and groan.*)

This is enough to end the conversation with Marge for some minutes because you don't know if the old man is mad or leaving the world. (*He sits up and resumes his natural voice.*) It doesn't matter what you want to do—this ghost persists. Most of the time one big eye is on you (*Demonstrates, then sits up again*) like witchcraft. You keep trying to remember if maybe you tracked mud into the house or maybe last Halloween you let air out of his tires or something. Makes you real jumpy.

The only thing to do is to get wise to this guy right away and leave the house entirely. Better a crust of bread at a hot dog stand where you can talk in peace about Life and Love than all the comforts of home with a ghost around rattling his chains.

Then there's the father who drives you completely nuts because he forgets he ever grew up. He's still back at Hampton Falls High School winning the game in the last fifty seconds with a hundred-yard runback of the kickoff. He's a little grey and fat around the belt, but he hasn't noticed it. He's still razzmatazz, go team go! He usually roams around wearing a baseball cap and carrying a football. It all happened in the Dark Ages, but to this dad it was only yesterday. Maybe he's that way because he hasn't done anything *since.*

You don't even have a chance to get a sweet smile from Marge before this old-timer is on your back. He slaps you on the back like a bone-setter looking for business. Then he goes on with his routine. (*Imitates father's actions and voice*)

"Hiya, old buddy-boy, old boy. How's everything in school? You in there slugging it out for old Hampton Falls, kid?

> 'Oh, Hampton Falls, dear Hampton Falls,
> Mother of men through the years . . .'

Yay, team! Say, did I ever tell you about that last game with Glens View Tech? We hadn't beaten Glens View in forty years, mind you. Forty long, lean years. Eh? Those were the days, buddy-boy, old pal. Giants walked the earth then, as they say. Not these puny delinquents you see around today. No offense meant. I know you're right in there fighting for the glorious green, George, old boy. Eh? Oh, your name is Ernie. O.K. What's in a name? as Lord Byron once said. Who? Shakespeare? I know. He said it too.

"Man, I used to take my banjo out in a canoe on Lake George, and we'd sing *real* songs. Not those jibber-jabber things you hear today. Stuff like . . . well, I forget, but really beautiful songs. A song had to have a melody, like 'Yes, We Have No Bananas' and 'Button Up Your Overcoat.'

"You should have seen me then, old pal. I was captain of the football team, captain of the baseball team, assistant captain of the track team, star of the basketball team, champion wrestler and weight-lifter. My grades? We didn't bother with grades in those days. But that last game against Glens View Tech was beautiful. I grabbed the kickoff (*He illustrates.*), I waited for my blockers . . . they didn't show up. The fans were screaming, especially all the beautiful girls. I got to the five . . . the ten . . . the fifteen . . . the twenty . . . (*He is running around, darting and weaving.*) At the thirty there were three big red players waiting for me. I sidestepped one . . . straight-armed the other and jumped right OVER the third . . . on to the forty, the fifty . . . the stands were going wild . . . banners were waving . . . the band was playing . . . 'Have Faith in Hampton Falls High.' I went over the goal line. The stands went mad. (*Holds up football*) This is the very football—I'm never without it. It leaks a little, but it's still good. Another time we were playing baseball against Saratoga. I was pitching . . ." (*He returns to normal voice.*) This fellow they can keep. He hasn't discovered that high school athletes today rank one rung above trained chimpanzees unless they're good students, too.

Then there's one more father. This fellow is slim, quiet, polite and has a good sense of humor. He treats you like an equal but not like a pal. He doesn't *want* to be your pal. He's a grown man and likes it that way. He tells you to make yourself at home, dig into the refrigerator if you're hungry, plenty of Coke if you're thirsty, play the hi-fi if you feel like it. . . .

Then, when his daughter comes into the room he says goodbye and walks out. You don't see him again all evening. He minds his own business.

He's the greatest.

I keep *hoping* I'll meet one like that some day!

THE END

4 | THE DOG SCHOOL

(This should be done by a stern, businesslike woman or man who is really touched only when the beauty of dogs comes up. She needs a desk and chair and a stern look when necessary. There should be a pencil and some sheets of paper available on desk. A sign reading DIRECTOR OF ADMISSIONS *may be used. The director ruffles around papers, looks up, smiles coldly, nods, stares again.)*

What is your name, please? Oh, Mrs. Twitchell. Which Twitchells are those? I see. The plain Twitchells. Well, there are Twitchells and Twitchells. We can't be too careful here at the California University for Dogs, you know. I believe I have your dossier here. . . . Well, my dear Mrs. Twitchell, it's merely your credit rating, your social rating, your Retail Credit report, your confidential insurance report, and various data our agents in the field have gathered.

(She bustles around through papers again.)

I don't seem to find your dog's history. What is his name again? . . . Richard the Lion-Hearted. Hmn. He doesn't look very lion-hearted. Ah, yes, here is his pedigree.

19

There's been some discussion about his admission. That's why it was in a special file. . . . Why? Did you say why? My dear woman, we don't permit every Rover, Ginger and Spots into our school. It's easier to get into Smith than it is to get into my school. . . . Yes, I'm very well aware a dog wouldn't *try* to get into Smith.

Joking about dogs is frowned on here, Mrs. Twitchell. Dogs are very sensitive about jokes. Notice how your Richard's ears are hanging. See the wounded expression in his eyes? . . . He what? He doesn't *want* to go to school? Don't be silly. He wants to go to school. He just doesn't know it. He doesn't want to grow up and bite mailmen and brush salesmen, does he? Does oo, Richard? Of course we don't. (*Makes cute motions at the dog*) When you get through dog school, Richard, you'll have a big advantage over other dogs. Do you know there are only half as many nervous breakdowns among educated dogs as there are among ignorant whelps?

I notice here in Richard's personality file that his grandfather had a little trouble. . . . You didn't know about that? His grandfather bit an internal revenue officer. This is a federal offense, in a way. At the best, it's not very tactful. . . . What was that? What difference does it make? Well, it makes a great deal of difference. Any scandal in a dog's family reflects on the dog.

We have some of the outstanding dogs in the country here, dogs from the best families. We don't want them all getting up at night, led by some rabble-rouser, and chasing cats or baying at the moon.

Richard's grandmother seems to have married, temporarily, at least, outside the Kennel Club's social register. Not a fatal flaw in a French poodle. In fact, not unexpected. Just the same . . . (*Stares over at Richard*) He has sense enough to hang his head.

(*She looks through papers thoughtfully.*) Well, the Board of Admissions is willing to take a chance on Richard the Lion-Hearted. On probation, of course.

(*She stares toward the dog again.*) He has a sort of wild look in his eye. Has he ever been known to consort with the left wing? The radicals? Russian wolfhounds and all that? . . . No? Hmn.

Now, I assume you understand that we can only do so much for the dog. We can train him. We can suggest a future goal in his life. We can teach him to be obedient and thoughtful. But the home is where the real learning is done.

Since your dog is to be a day student, he will be under his parents' control much of the time . . . *your* control, that is. You must do nothing to upset him or condition him badly. His homework will be important. You must help him with it. Most of the dogs who fail courses and cannot meet our academic standards do so because their owners do not help with homework.

There must be no letting him out of the house to hang around the street corner with bad influences. He must never be permitted to go wildly chasing squirrels or pigeons or anything of that sort. Above all, he must not be permitted to roam around in front of the house, darting out after trucks. There is some sense in chasing squirrels. Chasing trucks is a sign of low mentality. I mean, what could he do with a truck if he caught it?

Now, there must be no swearing or profanity while the dog is about. Dogs are very sensitive to bad language. If you burn a roast or bang your head on the cupboard door just restrain yourself. Say to yourself, "I must be calm or I may begin a neurosis in Richard. Could I ever forgive myself?"

Your what? Your husband swears a lot? I suggest you order him to stop or get another husband. This is a serious matter. He what? . . . He barks? You mean Richard barks at your husband? . . . Oh, your husband barks first. Has Richard ever bitten your husband? . . . I see. What did your husband do? . . . Bit him back, eh? Has he ever been to a psychiatrist? Eh? Not your husband, the dog. Beg pardon? . . . Oh, they've both been. Together? Oh, separately. It would have been better had they gone together. The more members of a family who go together, the better the results. Two heads shrunk are better than one, so to speak.

What were the results? . . . Your husband had a persecution mania and the dog had a trauma from having your husband make fun of the way he was clipped. Dear, dear.

Dear Mrs. Twitchell, you have a beautiful, purebred dog there. If your husband is interfering with the dog's happiness I certainly would not take long to make a choice. We shall do our best to produce a happy, well-balanced, educated, refined and serene dog, but when we have to fight against an uncooperative husband the odds are all against our success.

I think the least you can do is have the three of you sit around the dinner table some night and talk this thing out. Otherwise, in spite of our efforts here at the school you are going to have a very unhappy dog on your hands.

Have you thought of sending your husband to Dog-Haters Anonymous? It's a group of men who have a compulsion to snap at dogs, an inferiority complex in the presence of dogs. They get together once a week and talk over their dog-hating problems. Any time they are overcome with the desire to tease or kick a dog, they visit another member of Dog-Haters Anonymous and kick him instead. It works very well. . . . You don't think your husband's that far gone? Well, let us hope not.

I suggest, Mrs. Twitchell, that you bring him in here for a three-week stay, without letting him go home at all for that period. We'll have our psychologist look him over, and we'll give him a chance to get acquainted and adjusted. We'll put him on a special diet of bone meal, wheat germ, yogurt and Queen Bee Jelly. We'll give him plenty of rest. (*Pause*)

What, Mrs. Twitchell? . . . No, no. Not your husband. The dog. Yes. Our kennels aren't big enough for husbands.

Very well, Mrs. Twitchell. You bring Richard in tomorrow morning and we'll introduce him to everyone. I'm sure he'll be reconditioned nicely. Bring a check for five hundred dollars, too, for the first two weeks. This includes room, board, an hour a day on the couch, bones, nail clipping and medical care.

Very good, Mrs. Twitchell. Glad to have met you. Very happy to have met you, too, Richard the Lion-Hearted. We'll make a man out of you.

Good day. (*She stands there for a moment silently. Then she raises her hands in canine fashion and barks. In a moment she returns to normal and walks off smiling.*)

THE END

5 | THE REPAIRMAN COMETH

(Mrs. Rudolph, *a harried housewife, is expecting the plumber. She has been expecting him for several days. She is now on the telephone inquiring where he is.*)

(*Into phone*) Hello? Hello? Bright Star of the Morning Plumbing Company? What's that? Oh. This is Mrs. Rudolph of 64 Beechwood Grove. Yes. Three days ago I called for a plumber and you said you'd send him right over. An hour later when I called you said he was on his way. What? . . . He's still on his way? He only has to come half a mile. Eh? What's the matter? Water is dripping. Downstairs. I was standing there three days ago and plink, plink, plunk—cold drops dripped down on my head. . . . I did move out of the way. But that doesn't solve the problem. I put a pail under it and an old sweat shirt my daughter wore in high school. . . . What? Classical High School. Oh, yours went to Tech? That's nice. But the water still drips, plink, plink, plunk. I beg pardon? . . . You think I need a plumber. I *know* I need a plumber. I've been waiting for three days . . . All right, look it up. (*Pause. She taps her fingers nervously.*) Hello?

He's on his way, you say. Your best man. Good but slow, I'd say. Very well. But that water dripping—Oh, someone's here. Goodbye.

(*She turns from telephone and opens door to admit someone.*) Well, am I glad to see *you*. You stopped for lunch? That was three days ago. How long . . . Well, anyway, there's a drip right over here. See? Plink, plink, plunk.

It's not what? . . . It's not your problem? Oh, you're the TV man. That was a *week* ago. I had almost forgotten. I'm not getting any picture. There was this story last Saturday about a girl who wanted to marry this millionaire— but he was playing hard-to-get. Then she had a wonderful idea. She snapped her fingers—and then there was no picture.

(*She walks over and pretends to turn on TV set. She stands and waits.*) You think what? You think there's no picture? I could have told you that. What? . . . I agree with you. There *ought* to be a picture. Otherwise I could listen to the radio.

No, the tube isn't leaking. That's coming from the ceiling. I know I ought to get a plumber. Have you ever tried to get a plumber on Saturday? He comes Tuesday if you're a good girl and very, very quiet. (*She jumps back, startled.*)

What happened? You got a little shock? How long have you been working on TV sets? Your second job. You had a lot of schooling, you say? But they never told you not to touch a live connection with a screwdriver while standing in a puddle? You must have been absent that day.

(*She stands back and turns her head from side to side*

*as if she were watching him. Now and then she is startled
by some action of his.*)

What's that? I had this set a long time? No, I've had
it six months. You can what? You can get me a new set at
a discount? Glorious color? No, thanks. My husband says
most of the stuff is trash. I'd hate to make him watch
trash in color. Just fix this. You what? . . . You can't
fix it? Oh, you just take care of the sound. There's a special man who fixes the picture. Specialists, huh? Well, you
see that he gets here quickly. Goodbye.

(*She goes toward the door and then steps aside.*) Oh, I
imagine you're the plumber. You are? Well, welcome.
Have a nice trip? Did you come by boat? You just got
the call? They said at the office they sent you out days ago.
What? You just started working for them this morning.
Well, you're here, and that's a step forward. Just come
into the other room. (*She goes across the floor and stands
still.*) Feel anything? That's water. Cold water. It's dripping. You what? You suspect something's leaking. Good
for *you*. The bathroom is right above. Come.

(*She pretends to go up the stairs; turns.*) There we are.
Pink and gold. My husband hates it. Says it's sissy. But I
find it soothing. (*Her eyes seem to follow the plumber.
She starts, as he appears to be tearing at things.*)

Noisy job, isn't it? . . . You may have to pull up the
floor? And the linoleum, too? What's under there? Pipes?
Leaking pipes. Why did they have to put them under the
floor? That's the way they built this house. No, I'm not
blaming you. But what is it?

(*Motions as she talks*) The trap is over here, yes . . .
and the pipe coming from down there is over here . . .
and probably turns, and goes there. (*Pause*) Why does it

turn? Oh, so it can join the bathtub. I see. Then it turns over here to join the hot water and goes up there to the washbasin and then down again. Oh, into the wall and down under the floor.

How do you know all this, young man? Eh? What did you say? . . . Oh, you *don't* know. That's why you have to pull up the whole floor. Then what? You'll put in new pipes and everything will be fine? Who puts back the floor? A carpenter? That's nice. Why can't you put back the floor? Because you're a plumber. A splendid, forth-right answer. Besides, what? Besides, after the way you tear up the floor it can't be put back. I'll have to have a new floor? *Two* new floors? Why? . . . I see. A sub-floor and then a smooth floor. Why not just the sub-floor? . . . Because I'd get slivers in my feet. Then the inlay—of course. I what? I'll need a linoleum man to follow the carpenter to follow you?

You mean all this because of a few drops of water? Plink, plink, plunk. I *know* you didn't build the house. Don't keep telling me you didn't build the house. I know it's too late now to put the plumbing pipes out in the yard where it would be easy to get at them. You don't have to be sarcastic. (*Pause*) All right, start doing *some-thing*. Make a noise, at least, so my husband will think something is being done when he comes in. (*Pause*) I think he's here now. (*Looks at watch*) Where are you going? Oh, you've got to get some parts. How do you know what parts? . . . Oh, you have to get a crowbar to rip up the floor. All right. Let's go downstairs, then. (*She pretends to go downstairs.*) Don't fall and break a leg, now. I've waited days for you. (*Pause*) What would happen if I let the darn drip drip? What? The pipe would burst, the ceiling would fall, the walls would probably cave in and the plaster would come off. Well, I don't have much choice, do I?

Here we are. Hurry back. Oh, by the way, how did you ever happen to become a plumber? You what? You love it? Yes, I could see where you might, tearing up floors and smashing linoleum to bits. Hurry back. (*Steps aside*) Oh, I thought you were my husband. No. He's a much older man. You must be the refrigerator man. Oh, the garbage disposal. Of all people! It must be two weeks ago I called you. You were where? . . . In Maine, fishing? That's a nice place to be when my disposal goes *Geeeeek* . . . *Crash-sh-sh* . . . *Geeeeek*. My husband thought a jet plane had fallen into the yard, motor running.

(*She pretends to turn on the disposal unit.*) See? . . . It what? It may go into orbit? Very comical. But it does not dispose of what it is supposed to dispose of. And it's guaranteed. (*She stands back, nervously, with her hands to her ears now and then. After a moment she relaxes.*)

What? I certainly did not drop a baseball in there. Eh? Or a watch. What is that? The reverse camshaft is bent like an eggbeater and the franishaw is twisted over the . . . the what? . . . The cortisone? I see. Yes, it's very clear. The what? . . . Go on. The cycle is off? I see. It has to go back to the factory? A big job? Might explode? Hmn. How much? I mean an estimate. You estimate it at forty-seven dollars, but that's just an estimate? . . . The actual cost will be well over one hundred dollars. Why? . . . I see. Because that's how it goes. A fine explanation. They must have special courses in milking customers at all these technical schools. All right. Take it out. It's no good there.

Oh, here's the stove man. Come in. At last you're here. . . . You what? You were up in Maine, fishing. Must be quite a crowd of you up there. Can't be much room for the moose. Here's the stove. When I turn it on Low it comes on High. When I turn it to Broil the back burner goes on and the timer starts to ring. If I turn the front burner on, the oven door opens and a bell rings. . . . You do? Wiring problem, huh? Nothing serious? Don't have to rip up the floor? Don't have to send it back to the factory? Ceiling isn't going to fall down? Stove isn't going to blow up? I adore you! How much? (*Pauses and listens*) There's about two dollars worth of work but you'll have to charge me twenty-five because your wife is having a baby. Fine. Congratulations! I could hug you. At last I have met an honest repairman!

THE END

6 | SING A SONG OF SICKNESS

(A man is seated at a desk, addressing his associates. Occasionally he rises to demonstrate how his heart and other organs are affected by what he says and what he hears.)

Well, fellas, I guess you wonder why I, Sol Hokum, of the Hokum Song Publishing Company, called you fellas all in here. The trouble is we are in a rut. The trend is all toward sad, sick songs, and we are still punching out stuff like, "You're My Universe" and "Love Is the Jolliest Thing." That sort of stuff is out, fellas.

Songs need to have an earthy, sick flavor today. Somebody has to get a disease or break his heart or shoot himself dead or something. Now I open myself up to suggestions. What do you have to say, Herman? Uh? *(Listens)* "Now That I've Found You Again I Feel Worse Than Ever?" A good idea, Herman. But it doesn't have that rippling meter. Mull it over, Herman. Sleep on it. Sit on it. Put it down on the sidewalk and see if it walks.

How's that, Reginald? *(Listens)* "Stop Hitting Me, Darling, and Let's Talk It Over?" Hmm . . . Stop . . . hitting . . . me . . .

Too vague, Reggie. I like the hitting business, though.
Suppose we had something like "I'm Black and Blue From
Being Married To You." You get the implication? You
see the metrical possibilities?

I'm black and blue from being married to you,
You kick me around like a busted old shoe.
I'm bruised and I'm bent.
Why don't you repent . . .

I mean, something like that has a solid appeal to the
married group. It's real. It's like a Greek movie. Naturally, I'm just chopping these things off the top of my head
for you fellows to give them a transfusion and see if they
live. Understand?

How's that, Mannie? What? Let me have that again in
a clear, round voice. Hmm. . . "It's a Nice Night for
Coughing." Hmn. I don't see where you could go from
there, Mannie. I really don't. It's a nice night for coughing, so you cough. (*He coughs.*) Here you have to have a
special coughing arrangement in the music. Once you've
coughed, what happens? No, Mannie. Try harder.

How about you, Dan? Uh? Yep, I saw that one. What
was it? . . . That's right. (*Looks through some papers*) I
have it right here. "Have a Hard-Boiled Egg." It's not
negative enough, Dan.

Have a hard-boiled egg
Raise it high
To the sky
Up above,
If you're feeling sad and wistful
Why don't you try a fistful
Of hard-boiled eggs . . .

It's not exactly what I'm driving at, Dan. What I want is something terse and stark and a little sick. Like those studio cards. Let me think up on the spur of the moment something like what I mean. (*He pantomimes with great feeling while reciting this.*)

> I wish you were dead, dear,
> Or at least, pretty ill.
> You go to my head, dear,
> Because I'm in your will.
> You made me your heir
> And that's only fair
> But how can anyone so wealthy
> Keep on being so healthy?
> Please consider your heirs
> And fall down the stairs
> There to lie very still,
> While I wish you were dead, dear,
> Or, at least, very ill.

Of course that's a rough approximation of what is almost the sort of thing I nearly mean. It will have to be polished.

I guess that's all for now, fellas. Go back to work, and *suffer!*

THE END

7 | THE METHOD

(OLGA VETROW *is conducting a workshop in "The Method," that school of acting that has become so fashionable.* OLGA *is very keen on it.*)

We begin now to study acting. You think, maybe, acting is just saying lines. Nonsense. I say, nonsense. In acting we must learn to *be* what we are acting. No? Yes. Ah, but we do not begin by being Hamlet. We may never be Hamlet or Hedda Gabler. We must make a humble beginning. As with the acorn, so is it with us.

We must *know* what we are being. I do not mean we must murder somebody to be Hamlet. We must feel it here. (*She places her hand on her stomach then quickly shifts it to her heart.*) I have never murdered anybody—yet. So how do I know how it feels? I have murdered a horsefly. He is buzzing around like crazy. It is hot. You are tormented. No? Yes. The humidity it is 92. The feet ache. Oh, for some peace! Then comes the horsefly to make the world unbearable. He is buzzing, *buzzing, buzzing!* (*She makes a horsefly sound, then pretends to wave the horsefly away as it comes near. She becomes very fierce and cries out suddenly.*) Out, damnèd horsefly. I hate you. I kill you dead. (*With great venom and a loud smack she smashes the horsefly against her head. She picks up the fly and regards it with disdain.*) Pfui! (*With a leer she flings it away.*) Die! Die! (*She laughs hysterically. Suddenly she is calm.*)

We have all killed such a horsefly. To be a murderer on the stage all we must remember is the horsefly, and multiply it by a thousand. We cannot go around killing people for experience. We can kill horseflies.

But first we must learn to get inside small things. Not inside a murderer or a lover at first. Not even inside a horsefly. You see, before we know what it is to murder a horsefly we must know, how does a horsefly feel? So we begin with small things and we act them.

Now you, in the second row, stand, please, up. Are you *that* tall? We make another Gary Cooper from you, maybe. Or a Mr. Gunsmoke. Now I wish you to think of something and *be* it. Anything you think of. I will try and guess. You must convince me. (*She waits and watches, her finger under her chin, leaning her head from side to side, thoughtfully.*) You are, maybe, a baseball? . . . No? Hmm. A willow tree? No, you are not weeping enough. Well, what are you? A banana split? My dear boy, you did not convey a banana split to me. You are not melting and rich and covered with jellied pineapple. I did not get the picture.

You, the next girl—what is it? Linda? Be something for us, Linda. (*She watches again thoughtfully, pondering, turning head from side to side.*) You are a . . . well, I don't know. Is it necessary to be so . . . so . . . earthy?

You are maybe, a tin of sardines afraid of being opened? No? Hmm. . . . You are a banana afraid of being peeled? No? What are you? . . . A peaceful cow in the meadow? You did not suggest peace to me, Linda. You see how much we have to learn. So far we do not even know what it is to be a banana split or a cow. I will show you a cow. I am a cow. (*She gets down on her hands and knees and moos.*) Fresh milk! (*She waddles about, lifting and lowering her head.*) I am a sad cow dreaming of when I was young and won first prize in the fair. Can you see it in my eyes, and the forlorn way I wag my tail? I am *all* cow. I am so convincing if you gave me daisies I would eat them. I would enjoy them. Oh, moo moo! (*She stands up, smiling proudly.*)

Now, in the third row, Egbert. Be something. Anything. (*Once more she watches thoughtfully.*) An ostrich? There is a certain look in your eye of an ostrich. No? Peanut-butter sandwich? No, you have not made yourself look edible enough. What are you? . . . A lighthouse? Where is the shine from the top? Where is the roar of the breakers? No, you are not really a lighthouse. You just think so.

Look how I do it. Not a lighthouse, I am too short. But a dog. I am a French poodle so I bark in French. (*She gets down and barks "Alouette" for a moment. Then she looks up quickly, but remains on the floor.*)

Now I am a table. I feel wooden. I am groaning because they are putting heavy dishes on me. I have sad knots in my legs. I am a sad table who dreams of being four baseball bats and having some richness in my life.

(*She stands up suddenly, wilts, and throws out her hands to prepare to be a flower.*) I am going now into the soul of a flower. Goodbye. I am waiting for a bee to come. I am very beautiful, see? And colorful. And the bees love me.

Now, we run out of time. I assign the homework. During the week you will be a horsefly. Ladies will be lady horseflies and men, men. Just a simple, middle-class, urban horsefly. You will be also a folding table. Try to get the feeling of how it is to be dragged out and unfolded. Do these things constantly. Do not be bothered by what people think. Be a horsefly on the bus or at work among your fellows. They will understand. Be a folding table at lunch. Scream with the agony of being folded. Those of you who feel competent may try to be a horsefly *on* a folding table. This will be difficult but not impossible.

Now as we file out, let us all be horseflies. Bzzz! Bzzz! (*She buzzes around the stage and finally flies out.*)

THE END

8 | TOKYO TO NEW YORK

(This should be delivered by a man who wears glasses and is made up to look as Japanese as possible. He smiles forever and at anything, and has an air of both innocence and authority.)

Good evening, fellow Japanese preparing for to go to America. We begin this lecture with general ideas about America and funny people there. Some other time we go, one by one, speak of each thing more better. Is it?

First thing: American people all look alike and have funny names like Joe, Rock, Murphy, and Elvis. Not nice name like Fujiyama and Sukiyaki. Must get used. *Must* get used.

Boys and women hard to tell from each other. Both wear pants. Women wear short pants in summer, long pants in winter. Men wear long pants most time. Wear short pants to play golf. *(He pretends to swing a baseball bat)* Golf is game, also call gin rummy. Women's pants much tighter than men's. Is no reason for this. But is old saying in America, "Who wears the pants in the family? Everybody!" This call *togetherness*. To-geth-er-ness.

Family in U.S. not same as family in Japan. In Japan old people are wise and help young people. In America people over thirty are old-fashioned. If they give advice to young people, young people say, "Oh, ho ho! This went out in 1880!"

In U.S. father and mother must not strike child or punish very much because child will grow up to be bank robber or nut. This is theory in U.S. This theory very popular with young people. Not so popular with father and mother.

Young people in U.S. have magic words and make much witchcraft. This magic works so good, have phrase in America "boxed in" or "in a box." Young people use magic words and have parents in a box. One magic phrase is, "Get lost." Another is, "Don't be corny." Other phrases, "What am I, a baby?" and "All the others kids are going." When parents want children to do homework or wash dishes or such, children use magic words and then go play bop or twist.

Sounds like, "Wash the dishes and dust the living room, Brenda." Answer: "Ho, ho, get lost, don't be corny. I go boppy-bop. So long, whatsa matter, you think you J. Egbert Hoover?"

In U.S. children mostly run family. Is new idea. Must get used. Children have friends in living room, play rocky-rolly records . . . wah, wah, wah . . . thump, thump:

"You broke my teeth when you broke my heart, oh, ho, ho . . .

How can I smile now that we're apart, oh, ho, ho . . .

They say I'm too young to go steady
At eleven and a half,
Come on, twist again, say that's a laugh . . ."

Is like conjure up evils spirits and make rain or like cause
voodoo to fuddiddy-duddiddy parents. Parents must take
friends in cellar to play canasta because children using all
the room. Is new idea in America, easier to smile than fight.

Japanese have "losing face," is so, no? Also is in U.S.
but not all same. Mother call children, "Come to dinner.
Is hot. Is get cold! Hurry, hurry." Nobody come. Family
lose face if they come before they are call *three* times.
Many ways to lose face in U.S. Children get high marks
in school, lose face. Other children cry, "What is idea? You
show off? You got egg head?"

Egg head is very bad word in U.S. Anybody study hard,
work hard, learn very much, must keep it secret. You get
name Egg-Head and you must work hard to make people
think you rather play golf.

Must get used.

When fifteen or sixteen, children in America drive family car. Let parents use once a week. Is so. Pedestrian in
America is father or mother with teen-age children. Is
very so!

Children use magic words with car, like so: "Fillerup,
charge my old man." Is mean: Put gas in tank. My revered
parents will pay later. With cars also they have Rush
Hour. Here we have paradox. In Rush Hour nobody can
rush; everyone stand still in cars. But is call Rush Hour.
Must get used. One more magic word is, "No Parking."
This mean you park there and pray to ancestors that police
not notice.

Oh, so, is by the way a thought. Is very much magic word in U.S.: "Positively." Is funny joke. Positively no smoking. Positively no parking. Positively no loitering. What is mean this positively? Nothing. No smoking is no smoking. What is good, positively? Must get used.

Is interesting courtship in America. About thirteen, fourteen years old children start "go steady." Is like primitive initiation. Girl comes home and says, "Mama, Daddy, get the high heels, lipstick and perfume. I go steady now!" This means girl has entered magic circle by threatening a boy, "I beat your brains out!" if he does not go steady.

Must get used also to very strange American tribal dances: Bop and Twist. Bop is hop on the toe, come down on the heel and have expression on face of mystic contemplation with eyes half-shut and mouth hanging open. Twist is newer and not so mystic. (*He picks up a wide scarf and puts it behind him like a bath towel.*) To learn Twist rub obi or towel back and forth like drying back. Wiggle self much. Clap hands. Wiggle right knee in and then left knee in. (*He demonstrates.*) Now pretend to scratch back against wall, starting at neck and working down to base of spine. Aha, man! Well, all right! Get with it. Go, man, go!

Bop is much like Japanese wrestling. Hard to explain but I try. Please do not laugh as is very serious in U.S. I show you. Please pay attention right away. First thing people ask you in America is, "You bop? You twist?" If you say no you are out. No status. No face. Go hide somewhere. Stop the world and get off, as Americans say.

Here is bop. (*He hums a bop tune or a current rock and roll tune and dances around, in the style of an Indian war dance, giving out piercing war cries every now and then and shouting, "You wanna go steady, chick?" and "I way out far, babe!" When he is done he puffs and pants, smiling exuberantly.*) Is not bad when you get with it. Oh, so. Must learn.

Must finally end with a few words on American literature. Is not much literature in America. Is too busy watching TV and learning to cure dandruff and upset stomach. Two books are read very much. *Gone With The Wind.* Is very sad story about War of the Roses and shy little girl who loves Japanese soldier but cannot marry him. Also big thing is *The Catcher Coming Through the Rye.* Nobody knows what is about except all young people say is very important.

Most literature in America is what is call, Sick Cards. These are cards with funny pictures and strange message. Everybody sends to friends. But unlike Japanese who send little poem, or gentle idea of happiness, in U.S. is send drop-dead cards. Is so! If a friend is in hospital you send card that say, "I got sick all the same as you last year. I died." If friend is get married, send card, "Goodbye, old friend. You through." Is birthday? Your friend send card, "What did you expect? A gift, you cheap skate bum?" Is hard to explain reason for this. American ideas very funny but *must* get used.

Next lecture I explain more American customs and habits so when you go you get with it. Is so. No?

Meanwhile I say like in U.S., "So long, you bum. See you in funny papers!" (*Bows and exits*)

THE END

9 | MEET DOCTOR MARTIN

(This monologue is done by a woman. No props are needed. She is greeting her guests gaily.)

So nice to see you, Mr. and Mrs. Fitzel. So nice you could come to my little party. Yes, my thirty-eighth birthday. (*Laughs hollowly after a pause*) Yes, I have celebrated it *several* times. I rather like it. (*Clears throat angrily and turns*) Ah, Betsy and Herbie Reed. How nice you could come. . . . Dented what? Oh, the black car in front of the house. Don't let it bother you. It's my husband's old Chevrolet. . . . I'm so glad you could make it, Kay. Where's your husband? Oh, I'm so sorry he couldn't come.

(*Very effusively*) Why, Dr. Martin! How nice to see you. I hope it's a relief to get away from all those sick people. (*Turns aside to speak to maid*) No, thanks, Ruby, no canapés for me. Or cookies. My figure, you know. What's that, Doctor? . . . Yes, I have tried the baths. We have four of them, you know. It's a big house. My stomach acts up a lot, Doctor. Modern living. Pressure. Summit conferences, PTA elections, nuclear testing and all that. If they *knew* what it does to my digestion!

(*Reaches out as if to grab him*) No you don't, Doctor. All the guests have arrived, and we can have a nice chat now. It isn't often I find someone *simpatico* in our big neighborhood. You look so understanding. I feel a rapport has been established. Pardon? . . . Your wife? Oh, I'm sure she can take care of herself. Doctors' wives generally can. Ha ha! The shoemaker's children go barefoot. As they say in German, "Dos schoomuckers chilltren ees gung shbare-feets."

I hope you won't mind, Doctor, but you look so trustworthy, I can't help asking you—and please tell me if I'm being forward—but I get these pains in my stomach. . . . They start over here (*She illustrates the route of her pains as she talks*), then they climb up here for a while, and suddenly start up, swoosh!—and climb up here . . . then they circle around in back and go up my shoulder and down my tibia or whatever it is, until I get a cramp in my big toe. I take calcium wafers, alfalfa, wheat germ, multiple vitamins, spinach and just a teensy little pale green tranquillizer every day.

I'm on a low salt diet with very little cheating and I get seven hours of sound sleep when my husband doesn't snore. And I'm very active in ceramics and bird-watching. So I'm *sure* it's not mental. Every time anyone has a tummy ache these days it's supposed to go back to their childhood when they stole a dime from Mummy's piggy bank. But I couldn't *get* anything out of Mummy's piggy bank. I mean, I'm mentally utterly empty . . . of guilt, I mean.

Then I get twinges in my southern iliac, especially when I'm holding a good hand of bridge. (*Pause*) I hope I'm not boring you, Doctor. Oh? Oh, *that's* your wife. (*Unim-*

pressed) Well, she *does* look as if she'd be a big help washing syringes and all that. Now, about these pains: they seem to occur whenever I eat strawberries or smoke mentholated cigarettes. They're accompanied by a sort of wheezing. (*She wheezes to illustrate—very effective and dramatic wheezes, a little like the horn on a Diesel locomotive.*)

I've looked at my tongue and it looks all right. I mean, it looks like a tongue. Nobody's tongue is her best feature. Ha ha. I get these migraine headaches when . . .

What was that, Doctor Martin? You what? Oh, well, imagine that. Of course! Why not? You're an *animal* doctor not a . . . well, what would you say . . . not a *people* doctor. Ha ha. The joke certainly is on me. I've always admired animal doctors. As they say in German, an animal can't tell you what his symptoms are and, well. . . .

Look, Doctor, I have this dog, Jean Jacques Rousseau— we call him Spike for short. Spike isn't well. For example, when we tell him to sit up and beg he rolls over, and when . . . what, Doctor? Oh, an emergency at the cat hospital? Well, I'm so sorry to see you go so early. Parties are *such* fun.

THE END

10 DON'T GET NERVOUS

(JOHN CHRISTOPHER, *a young husband, is wearing an apron and tidying up for his wife who is ill. She is stretched out on a sofa in the living room, which leads into the kitchen.* JOHN *goes back and forth as necessary. A stepladder, broom, pitcher, and telephone may be used.*)

Now, Brenda, I don't want you to worry about a thing. The doctor said you should get plenty of rest, and, above all, no worrying. It's all nerves, you know. . . . What, dear? Yes, I know you sprained your ankle. I meant that. (*Fusses around where she is resting, pulling up blanket and settling pillow*) Oh, you want the blanket down there? Not up here? I was just trying to make you comfortable. I know you think I'm lazy and careless sometimes, but when my back is up against the wall, I come through. . . . What, dear? The pillow? I just fixed it for you. (*Looks pained, but carries on*) No, you're not hurting my feelings. I always look this way when I'm trying to help. Concern shows on my face. (*Adjusts pillow*) How's that? . . . Good.

What? A cup of weak tea? Oh, you need more than

that. You need something substantial, something to build you up, something to take care of those frayed nerves. What, dear? . . . An ocean voyage? Did Dr. Smetna say that? It's easy for him. I wish we could afford an ocean voyage. I wish we could afford a good, sturdy canoe.

Yes, dear, I know Dr. Smetna takes a cruise every year. I think I pay for most of it.

What? What cobweb? Way over there? I must say, darling, there is not one thing wrong with those beautiful blue eyes of yours. No, sir. Not when you can see a cobweb from a prone position, fifteen feet away.

Don't get up! It's not an emergency. Even a *young* husband can take care of a cobweb. I'll get the broom . . . or something. (*Goes to kitchen at side of stage. Calls out*) Where do we keep the broom, dear? Behind what? Oh, the stove. Oh, yes . . . the little ladder? The aluminum one. Yes. (*Comes toward her*) Here it is, dear. At your service. Just keep calm. We'll get that nasty old cobweb. (*Speaks softly, to himself.*) Stepladder, topped with books. old magazines, towels—that's not what a stepladder is for.

(*Moves things around trying to find a place for them*) The sink isn't the place for it, either, but . . . (*Louder*) I'm coming, dear. Calm yourself. I know it must be terrible to lie there staring at a cobweb, but it isn't as if the roof were leaking or wasps were coming out of the fireplace. What, dear? (*Carries ladder and broom toward wife*)

Huh? Talking about wasps in the fireplace makes you nervous? Oh, darling, I'm sorry. Musn't get nervous. That's the one thing Dr. Smetna insists on. Serenity. Calmness. No wasps in the fireplace. No bats, no mice. Nothing.

Now, here we go! Death to cobwebs! (*Straightens lad-*

der and climbs it) Where is it? I don't see it. Over where? Oh. (*Gets down from ladder and moves it over a few feet, climbs it again. Waves broom around, topples, with broom waving. Falls against wall.*)

Don't get nervous, dear. No damage done. The cobweb is gone. What? So is your blue vase? You know that vase was an eyesore. Yes, I'm aware your dear mother gave it to us, bless her and her many gay contributions to our life together, but, really, it was ghastly. I mean, all those dragons and things . . . (*Rubs his back and limps a little as he moves toward his wife*)

Now, don't cry, dear. I can't bear to see you cry. Well it can't be helped. The cobweb's gone, isn't it? One thing at a time, dear. That's what caused you to get into this run-down condition. You try to worry about everything at once. Try to worry about one thing at a time. Now we've worried about the cobweb and the vase your mother gave us, let's start on something else.

What? Oh, the flowers. No, I didn't water them. I can't think of everything. Please, dear, don't cry again. I'm not shouting. I'm just articulating clearly. (*Articulates slowly so as to illustrate*) "See the cat. The cat has a tail. Oh, what a big tail the cat has!" It's just speaking clearly, that's all. Not shouting. (*Goes to kitchen and returns with pitcher of water*) What's that? What crack? Oh, in the ceiling? It's been there a long time. Well, you never lay there looking up before. As soon as you start moving around, it'll go away. Ha ha. What, dear? No, I can't plaster the ceiling right now. I've got to water the flowers. (*Comes toward her. Telephone rings and startles him.*)

The telephone! I'll get it. Don't you try to move, dear. I know how vital the telephone is, but I'm quite capable of

answering it. (*Rushes toward phone and answers it*) Hello?
Who? Oh, yes. Marge Fuddle. Well, she's coming along,
Marge. Yes. Canasta? Oh, not for a while yet, I'm afraid.
No excitement. No screaming and shouting and hair-pull-
ing. Ha ha. Nothing like that. Doctor's orders. Just rest,
peace, quiet. What? Yes, she is out of touch. Uh? (*Shifts
uneasily back and forth, making faces, nodding and sighing
as he listens to Marge. Takes phone off his ear and pats ear
tenderly. Finally he hangs up.*) Yes, Marge. Thanks a lot,
Marge. Good to hear from you. What, dear? (*He is startled
again.*) Don't scream like that, my angel. Keep calm.
What? The water pitcher? It's a priceless antique? Oh, your
dear mother. Well, I'm not harming it. It holds water. Or
maybe it doesn't. I've been feeling a funny, wet trickle.
. . . All right, dear, I won't use it. (*Starts toward kitchen,
bumps against something*)

Don't scream again, dear. Bad for your nerves. No, I
didn't break it. Just a little chip. Not even a chip. See?
All right, I'll put it away carefully.

What? Marge? Oh, she said . . . well . . . McGiffen's
is having a sale of curtain rods . . . uh . . . Mazie Heffer
is letting her hair grow. It's at that awkward stage where
you can't put it up . . . uh . . . Ethel Fitzhugh has dyed
her hair purple . . . or violet . . . the canasta group
can't agree on what show to see with the kitty money . . .
that's about all I can remember. (*Pause*) I *know* there was
more. It'll come back to me.

Now, let's just relax. I'll get you something to eat. Boy,
I'm getting a little tired and nervous myself. So much
running around . . . so many things to think of . . .

A cup of weak tea? Oh, of course not. I'll make you a real
good dinner: lamb chops, baked potatoes, early June peas

—just you wait a little. I guess you never knew I could cook, eh, honey? Oh, it won't make you sick. It's what you need. You can't live on weak tea. You can't get your strength back and your nerve ends padded up with weak tea. Just leave it to me, darling.

(*Moves to kitchen*) First pre-heat the oven . . . set gas at 350 or 500 or something . . . hmm . . . (*He starts humming as he bends down and opens oven door. Turns on oven and feels in pocket for matches*) Matches . . . matches. . . .

(*Feels around top of stove, and finally finds matches.*) Ah! Matches. (*Sings*) "Bringing in the sheaves . . . bringing in the sheaves . . . we shall come rejoicing . . . tum-tee-tum-tee-tum . . ."

(*Pretends to light match. There is an explosion. He backs away suddenly, putting his hands up to his face.*)

What, dear? (*Staggers wearily to wife*) No. No, dear. Now don't get hysterical. No, it isn't war. Just a little accident anyone could have. What eyebrows? Oh, those. No, darling. Now be calm. I lit the gas and didn't have a match right away, and, ha ha, boom-boom, ha ha. No, dear, the door is still on the oven—it's just bent a little. (*Weaves dizzily and speaks weakly*) Move over, dear. I think I'll lie down a few minutes myself. Then I'll make us both some weak tea. (*Lies down on sofa*)

THE END

11 | FIRST DANCE

(This touching item should be done by a woman. She may use a large handkerchief to twist around and a large clutch bag, bulging. A chair would also be helpful. None of these is necessary, though. They can be simulated. Keep in mind that the character portrayed is utterly flustered, and everything, practically, is vital.)

Do you recall your first dance? Probably you were in junior high. You would be, today, anyway. You had your first real prom dress, stretched out stiffly with crinolines, probably. You hardly dared to sit down. You had real high heels and your mother had let you use a dab of her expensive Arpège or Miss Dior or something. You felt terribly grown-up, didn't you? You also felt, at times, awfully childish, too.

You had to wait for your date, of course. Boys were more casual about dances. They were scared and shy, too. Actually they would rather be playing basketball or hockey. You never knew whether or not they were going to bolt at the last minute. It was a terrible suspense.

And, naturally, they were never on time.
It went something like this, didn't it?

I'm *not* nervous, Mother. Don't keep *telling* me I'm
nervous. Maybe you weren't nervous at your first prom.
Maybe you were twenty-two years old before you went to
your first prom. In the old-fashioned days that's how it was.
I know. I saw *Gone with the Wind* twice. Daddy, please, I
will not sprain my ankles. I've worn heels before. I prac-
ticed all day, anyway . . . What, Mummy? Of course I can
dance in them. Anyway, we dance in our stockings. . . .
Why? What a question! Because our feet hurt. Natch!

We don't dance really, anyway. The boys can't dance.
Their feet hurt, too, I guess. Maybe they never learned.
. . . What? We sit and talk. . . . About what? I don't
know. We drink Coke and talk.

Daddy, please, you're getting me all excited. The dress
is perfectly all right. I'll hold it up. What do you mean,
am I sure it's just Coke? (*Listens, astonished*)

You think it would be nice if you and Mummy came
and chaperoned? Oh, Daddy! Don't even mention it. I'd
die. I'd die right then and there. People would think I was
a child. How can you have any fun with your own parents
there? They don't understand. How *could* they understand? . . . Of course I love you. I think you're both
quaint. . . .

Oh, Daddy, no, not the lecture, not the long one about
virtue and taste and unspoiled youth and all that. No,
Daddy, please. Some other time. Some rainy night in
September. . . .

I know, Mummy. A girl has to be careful. I know. I'm
told ten times a day. After the prom? I don't know, Daddy.

Probably Joe's Pizza Palace on the Turnpike. It is *not* a dive. It has the best pizza in town and all the kids go there. (*Pause. Looks horrified*)

Eleven o'clock? Mummy, you can't mean it. The dance isn't over until midnight. Then we go to Joe's Pizza Palace. Mother, there is nothing immoral about pizza, even at one in the morning. Pizza is a traditional American dish after a prom. Daddy! Do you want me to be a white penguin? Avoided? Shunned? Way down in the pecking order?

I'll die if I have to be home before the other kids. I'll simply die. I'm not going to be kissing anybody. I couldn't bear to kiss Jimmy. Mummy, we do *not* use the word necking. If he kisses me good-night it will be on the forehead. I know Jimmy. We will just eat pizza and stare at each other.

(*She glances at her watch nervously.*) It can't be quarter of nine. What time do you have, Daddy? . . . Ten to nine? Mummy? . . . Five to nine! What time *is* it? Oh, I'll die. Mummy, he was supposed to come at eight-thirty. He swore he'd come at eight-thirty on his Eagle Scout's honor or something. Because I told him if he was not here at eight-thirty he'd get my handbag over the head. . . . What, Mummy? The clocks can't all be fast.

Mummy? What if he has mumps? Oh, I'd die. Mummy, remember his little brother Corby? Last week he had mumps. Remember we laughed about it? How little we knew. Remember I called Jimmy every day to see if he was healthy? I told him to avoid his brother. *Shun* him, I said. I told Jimmy to be careful crossing streets and to get to bed early and not risk indigestion or anything. Oh, if he is stricken with something I'll die.

Mummy, remember three years ago when I was a baby?

I shot at Jimmy with a water pistol full of red ink? Mummy . . . Mummy, you don't believe he's been wait͏ing all this time for revenge?

What if he's had an accident? His father drives wildly. What if Jimmy is dangling from a maple tree on Pineywoods Avenue and we're all sitting around here as if everything were going to come out fine?

We're ostriches! We're just lulling ourselves. He's in the hospital. I can feel it. I heard an ambulance go by an hour ago. I can feel it. Or he's got the mumps. Oh, Mummy, I'm not crying. I'll kill him. Can't he be in an accident some other time? Can't he have the mumps next summer? My first real ball and—

(*Suddenly, starkly*) He is not coming. I'm finished. I can never face the gang again. Never. I will enter a monastery. Or a convent, I mean. I won't break. Don't worry. I will withdraw from the world. Like Florence Nightingale. I'm transferring next week to some convent where they teach nursing. I'll do good. People will wonder why a young and healthy girl like me should withdraw from the world and shun men—except sick men. I'll be pale and sad and mysterious, and no one will ever know my secret.

I'm quitting school Monday. I shall never be able to face society again. Not after this heartbreak. Not after this snub. Oh, I can hear them laughing in Joe's Pizza Palace. Anne Hathman has been stood up! Ha, ha, ha, ha! Little do they know. . . .

Daddy, Mummy, don't try to change my mind. I knew this would happen. I'm not hysterical. I'm perfectly calm. . . . *What?* . . . I can't quit school? They'll arrest me? Ho, ho. I'll go on a hunger strike. I'll be emaciated and sickly and weak and tottering, like a fashion model. . . .

What? Don't call him. *Don't*, Daddy. Let me wither away by myself. There's no use. I am doomed. Daddy! Please. Mummy, he's on the phone! I specifically asked him not . . . Oh, well, it doesn't matter any more. My life is over. Jimmy has deliberately exposed himself to the mumps. I know it. I'll show him. When I'm a missionary in the Congo and Jimmy comes in bleeding from the jungle, he will recognize me suddenly and then he will say, "Anne, forgive me. I have always loved you." But it will be too late. I will look at him pityingly and say, "Whatever was once in my heart has died long ago." I will say . . .

What, Daddy? What?

Jimmy has gone skating? I'll *kill* him. I'll strangle him. I'll . . . *Skating!* (*Pause*)

I . . . what? What, Mummy? Oh. (*Numbly*) Oh, the dance is *Saturday?* And this is *Friday?* Oh . . .

Fine parents I have. Fine parents. They let me go on thinking it's Saturday when it's Friday. . . . What? You thought the dance was on Friday? Well, it isn't. And he won't come Saturday, either, I'll bet. He'll have the mumps, or break his leg, skating. Why does he have to risk injury the night before our date? People have no consideration. I'm *not* hysterical. (*Pause*)

Was there any pecan pie left from dinner? I need nourishment to bear up. (*Exits bravely.*)

THE END

12 | NAMING THE BABY

(The following piece is best done by a man. Fathers seem to have more trouble with naming babies than mothers have—probably because fathers feel they ought to do something. No props are necessary except a book which supposedly contains given names.)

I've been thinking about a name for the baby, dear. I mean, I believe that even though it's some time away, it's never too early to think. People often name babies in a hurry, you know, and they come up with something suddenly, like . . . well . . . Vladivorginskia, which means, "little fellow with the bent nose" in Russian. I just mention that as an example. . . . You what? . . . You have it all planned? But, my dear wife, I think you ought to give *me* a chance. . . . It what? . . . It doesn't matter what I think? I know you didn't say that unkindly. You're not yourself these days, naturally. Uh? I know, but listen to me first, will you? That's all I ask. Then we'll hear from you.

Junior is out, of course. Juniors have a hard time. People call them Junior. I would like my name perpetuated . . . Grover Taft Coolidge Cadwellington. It never did me any harm. They just called me "Cad" in college. . . . Uh? Oh, it was a joke. Ha ha.

William is a good, square name. Bill. What, dear? . . . Too dull, and besides, what if it's a girl? We'll come to the girls later. I have a book here, *Don't Name Your Child in Haste*. It has all the boys' names first and then the girls'.

At random I find Hahawi . . . it means rain clouds in Cherokee. It *is* odd, but it certainly is distinguished. Harold . . . powerful warrior. . . . What? . . . He might be a tennis player, or a bookkeeper? Yes, we have to find something that will fit nearly all circumstances, something crisp and clear. (*Pause*) Granite? Granite Cadwellington? Too hard? Yes, I guess so. Asbestos? It's from the Greek, meaning fireproof. I think it's silly, myself, but I happened to think of it. (*He looks through the book.*)

Ephraim? It means very fruitful. He might run an orchard when he grows up. Furman . . . it means cheesemaker. . . . What, dear? Well, I just happen to be sentimental. I know how you love cheese. Calvin . . . that means bald. That's not very hopeful, is it?

When you come to think of it, there *aren't* many names to give a baby—I mean safe and sane names. Marvin . . . means beautiful sea. . . . Lionel means little lion. (*Pause*)

They just do not have any up-to-date, modern names. Everything means "beautiful meadow" or "bright in fame" or "down in the dell." They don't have anything that means six-cylinder sports car or jet flight, or one-who-pays-his-income-tax-honestly—nothing like that. . . .

What, dear? I know you wanted to say something but let me just take a look at the girls' names. I mean, I paid $3.95 for this book.

Let's look up **Nedra**—I always liked that. Nedra . . . hmm . . . vicious **viper?** Extraordinary! Why would anybody name a kid Vicious Viper?

Beulah means married. What good does that do a baby? Probably isn't thinking about it until she's twelve or so. Say, what about Callista . . . most beautiful. Huh? . . . Sounds like a patent medicine? Callista for acid stomach. Yes, it does, at that. (*Thumbs through book again*)

Hey, look at these—Hazel, Fern, Heather, Brier, Ivy, Myrtle, Petunia, Rose, Laurel. What wonderful names for a landscape gardener with nine daughters. I wonder why girls have plants' names. Do boys have? Oak? Crabgrass? Chestnut? No. Leah . . . that means weary. I wouldn't call anybody weary before she *starts!*

I have it! Jeanie. (*Sings*) "I dream of Jeanie with the light brown hair. . . ." That's it. (*Pause*)

I'm what? I'm wasting my time? Why? . . . Letter from whom? Uncle Messmore? What does that old goat have to do with it? That tiresome windbag never writes unless it's to criticize—a man with millions who can't think of anything better to do than shoot off his big fat mouth. . . .

I *am* listening, but anything *he* has to say cannot possibly interest . . . *What?* Read that again. (*Pauses to listen intently*) Trust fund of one million dollars? Say that again. (*Nods as he listens*) One million dollars if the child is named Messmore.

What? A postscript? (*Pauses and speaks slowly, following his wife*) If it chances to be a girl it shall be named . . . Messmorina. Messmore . . . Messmorina . . . they have a lovely sound, don't they, dear? A lovely, glittering, clanking sound, a nice ruffly sound, too. Messmore Cadwellington? It rings, doesn't it? Like a cash register. . . .

What, dear? People will call him Messy? I suppose, but
. . . What, dear? It's a heavy load to bear—ha ha—but a
million dollars will make it a lot lighter, a *lot* lighter!
(*Shakes head emphatically as he exits*)

THE END

13

THE GREENFIELD AFRICAN VIOLET CLUB

(*A serious and ladylike matron, the chairman of the club, is sitting at a table, presiding over a meeting. She looks over her spectacles constantly. On the table are assorted memos and papers, as well as a glass of water from which she drinks occasionally. There should be a wilted or scraggly group of African violet plants on the table, too. The chairman looks down the hall, over her glasses, in annoyance, and then bangs her gavel in a ladylike fashion.*)

Attention, *puleeze!* Mrs. Caliwell, if you will, please? Order.
(*She waits a moment, looking around. She stares vaguely at the plants on the table and then, half-interested, pours a little water from her glass into the saucers of the plants.*)
Order. *Order!* (*Pause*) That's better. (*Smiles*) I hereby declare the monthly meeting of the Greenfield African Violet Club open. Our club is ever growing, ever expanding, always seeking new horizons. In fact, there is an idea I want to throw out to you about changing our name to the African Violet and World Affairs Club. What with the world situation being the way it is, I thought we should

all try to understand how closely African violet culture is tied up with world peace and prosperity. No nation that does not cultivate African violets can long endure.

African violet lovers are exponents of peace. Not that they are for peace at any price. They will fight, if need be, for the freedom to cultivate their own varieties; they will defend themselves to the end, with watering cans and trowels.

There has been some talk . . . I think Miss Gardiner brought it up . . . that with the terrible situation in Africa, we should protest by changing the name to heavenly violets or American violets, but I think this would only add to the confusion in the world. Lord knows there's enough confusion now.

On the other hand, we must make progress. We must stay contemporary. Mrs. Kirkeby, whom you all know as the author of an article in *Flower Lovers Monthly,* "Should African Violets Be Sent to the Moon?" is arranging a nice little meeting at her home this spring, to discuss the possible effects of weightlessness on African violets. (*She turns to the potted plants rather wistfully.*) Mrs. Frank Elderberry, who is confined to her home with a touch of falling over a hose in the greenhouse at Belchertown, kindly sent us an example of a new and rare variety, Ruffled Mrs. Kennedy, a variation of Double Mrs. Truman that Mrs. Elderberry grew so successfully. I'm afraid the dry air has not been too good for them, but when they are placed in their proper environment I feel sure we shall all be proud of Mrs. Elderberry.

I'm afraid none of the regular officers are here today. (*She looks around vaguely.*) I'm afraid the Bingo game at Thompsonville has drawn quite a few of our members.

Although I hope not the treasurer. Ha ha. I'm sure you understand that as a joke. Mrs. Crunk is a dear Smith College pal of mine and we have grown our African violets together since dormitory days. In fact, Elsie wrote her master's thesis on The African Violet and Juvenile Delinquency.

I do have the treasurer's report here. (*Looks through papers*) . . . I think . . . Hmn . . . Elsie's recipe for old-fashioned yeasty wheat cakes seems to have been mixed up with . . . uh, well. . . . Oh, here it is. "Be sure to get my shirts from the laundry. You and your African violets! You don't even have time to. . . ." (*Laughs uneasily*) Oh, dear, that's a note from my dear husband. His bark is worse than his bite. Hmn. Now, here we are. Dues to date, fifty-two dollars. Profit from rummage sale, one dollar.

(*The chairman sighs and smiles sadly.*) Well, if you people are going to buy the nicest things for a song—I mean before the regular customers *get* there—we can't expect to . . . Well, I'll get to that later.

Profit from fudge sale: loss, one dollar.

Here is another case where we are not giving our all. If we are going to sell fudge in the schools during voting hours, we can't eat it all ourselves. That's what my husband calls simple economics.

So . . . uh . . . Miscellaneous expenses, fifty-four dollars. Let's see, two and one are three . . . (*She draws figures in the air.*) none to carry . . . minus one. . . . Our net balance is fifty-two dollars minus fifty-four. (*She waits a minute, puzzled, and then does some figuring in the air again.*) It can't be done, can it? We show a profit of minus two dollars. Well . . . ha ha . . . when you consider the government's deficit that's not bad at all. That amounts to about two cents per African Violet member.

Our dear secretary, Phoebe Pillaster is in absentia—she isn't here, that is. I believe she is distributing African violets to the shut-ins at the York Street Prison. But I *do* have the minutes. (*Picks up a paper. Looks at it from several angles*) Yes. (*Laughs uneasily*) She wrote it on the back of a menu from Ye Little Violet Tea Room. (*Pause while she examines paper*) With your permission I shall read it. I was just wondering how watercress and peanut butter sandwiches with yogurt got into our minutes. (*Reads*)

"The regular monthly meeting of the Greenfield African Violet Club was held last Thursday afternoon at the GAR Hall with sixty-two in attendance. It was moved, seconded and carried that we have our annual banquet at the Whole Wheat Organic Restaurant in Sturbridge. The motion to invite the husbands to attend was voted down by a vote of fifty-two to nine.

"It was unanimously carried to send ten dollars to Herbie Reed's greenhouse for the accidental destruction done by the chairman's dog to the African violets we were inspecting on our last field trip. The motion was amended by the treasurer to read, 'When we get it.' Mrs. Fossingham showed us several cactus plants she and her husband collected on their trip to Las Vegas. She explained the various spiny ones, and a vote of sympathy was extended to her when she sat on one.

"It was moved and unanimously approved that we appoint Ethel Sturgess a committee of one to draft a letter to the Postmaster General suggesting an African Violet commemorative stamp. The chairman pointed out we have honored basketball, cherry blossoms, electric light bulbs, the poultry industry and dozens of other uninteresting things, so why not the African Violet, which is the very heart of America?

"The meeting closed with the usual prayer." (*She puts down paper.*)

I move the minutes be accepted. Seconded? Right. All in favor? Carried.

Our last bit of business is a suggestion by me that we send a strong letter of protest to the Soviet Premier warning him that the Greenfield African Violet Club, affiliated with the Greater New England African Violet Club, is strongly opposed to his actions. Seconded? Right. Those in favor? Aye? No? Ayes have it. Motion carried. Will Mrs. Goshall, who, as we all know, is the author of the recent *African Violet Murder Case,* please draw up a letter for us —and don't spare the adjectives. Ha ha. Thank you.

I regret very much that the two speakers scheduled to be here today were unable to appear. This will . . . ha ha . . . give us a chance to get home in time to cook our husbands' dinner for a change.

The Princess Margaret, whom we hoped to have here today to talk on African Violets and the British Empire, did not answer our invitation. The Prime Minister was also unable to be with us, probably because of duties elsewhere. Next week we hope to have the Vice-President talk to us on My Life, Romance and African Violets. We haven't heard from him just yet. But he *is* in this country.

I believe that's about all. I move that the meeting be adjourned. Favor? Aye? No? Meeting adjourned.

See you next month. Meanwhile: Keep Your Pots Moist!

THE END

14 DON'T FORGET

(MR. CRANSHAW, *director of the Cranshaw Memory School, is sitting behind a desk that conceals him below the waist. He is interviewing a new student.*)

Good morning, Mrs. Hollis. I'm happy to see you here at the Cranshaw Memory School. Remember our motto. What is it again, now? Oh, yes. If Cranshaw Can't Teach You To Remember You Might as Well Forget. Made it up myself.

Sit down, Mrs. Hollis. Memory is the most important thing the brain possesses. Without memory we would forget things. Any brain can be trained to remember things. It's all a matter of stimulating the medulla obligato and tickling the Isle of Capri which is located on the South Shore of the mid-brain or, as we call it medically, the octopus.

Now, a failing memory can ruin your life. A friend of mine laughed at my memory course—old Herbie Reed; one day he forgot and put the sugar in the freezer. His wife put him in the freezer. Another friend of mine, Charlie Swann, got married to a woman he despised because he forgot to say No. I even know some people who forget to get dressed in the morning. Of course, they're pretty far gone. All of which proves you simply can't afford to forget.

My course, Mrs. Hollis, is foolproof. I use the connecting method. One thing leads to another in life. In order to remember, all we have to do is connect things together. See? . . . You don't see? Hmm.

All right. Let us assume you are to meet your husband at Petticoat Lane and Main Street at 12 o'clock. On the way you intend to purchase one half-gallon of strawberry ice cream, six frankfurters, six doughnuts, and a new hat. Got that?

What? . . . You wouldn't *try* to remember it, you'd make out a list? No, you wouldn't. You'd forget the list. In fact you'd forget to *make* the list. You'd get down the street and (*Imitates the action*) say, "Oh, good heavens, I was supposed to do something. What *was* it!" Then you'd fuss around a while and finally go to the dentist, with whom you had an appointment next week . . . and anyway it wasn't the dentist, it was the dog hospital. You see? I know. . . .

No, Mrs. Hollis, you do *not* make a list. I once made out a laundry list—before I became the world's greatest memory expert—and instead of sending it to my Chinese laundryman I sent it to the grocery store. I had chop suey for six months, with the buttons sewn on free. Terrible thing.

No, Mrs. Hollis, you use the connecting method. You visualize . . . you *imagine* how these things look. You see a petticoat for Petticoat Lane. You picture a half-gallon of strawberry ice cream, wrapped in the petticoat. What kind

of petticoat? . . . (*Tartly*) What kind would you like?
. . . Something with black lace in a size 36? It doesn't matter what kind. Now we have the ice cream and in the ice cream we stick six frankfurters. How's that? . . . You don't *like* frankfurters and ice cream? You don't *have* to like them. You just think of them. Six little frankfurters stuck in the strawberry ice cream, and on top of the frankfurters, what? . . . No, not mustard and relish. You must be hungry. Did you forget breakfast? No, on top of the frankfurters—a doughnut. A doughnut ring around each frankfurter like a ringer in horseshoes or an engagement ring, and finally, the new hat.

Do you understand? This is important. Now, let me see if you have remembered. Go ahead. . . . What black slip? It's a petticoat. Come, come, now, Mrs. Hollis . . . think. Ice cream . . . ice cream . . . does that send up a chain of memory? Come now . . . ice cream . . . husband . . .

You what? . . . You are going to meet your husband in a black lace nightgown at the Strawberry Cafe and play horseshoes? No, no, Mrs. Hollis. Think again. The ice cream is melting. You are going to meet your husband . . . (*Listens*) at Petticoat Lane . . . right . . . and on the way (*Listens*) you are going to stick six horseshoes in the ice cream with mustard and relish and get a new hat.

Well, that's a start, Mrs. Hollis. At least you remembered the new hat. That will be all for the first lesson. (*Pauses*) Just a moment, Mrs. Hollis. You forgot my fee of ten dollars. We must work hard at remembering, Mrs. Hollis? Eh? . . . You forgot to bring your pocketbook?

Mrs. Hollis, you *are* in a bad way. I recommend you

come twice weekly, at least, and never forget your pocket-book. I'll mail you a bill. . . .

Oh, yes, I'll show you to the door, Mrs. Hollis. The Cranshaw Memory School, the school that never forgets, is glad to be useful. Just step this way. . . . (*When he gets up from the desk, he is wearing bright-colored shorts because he has forgotten to put on his trousers!*)

THE END

15 | THE APPRECIATION OF MUSIC

*(This can be done by a man or woman. He (or she) needs no props, but if a phonograph playing a wild, thunderous Wagnerian passage or anything ear-splitting is available, it would be more fun. A record can be marked so that the needle goes down on the proper passage. Otherwise the actor can pretend he has a phonograph and pretend to listen. He might also hum, or give vent in some audible way, to noisy chords—*pum pum. . . . ta da *dee* pum-pum-pum—*the way many music lovers try desperately to do.)*

I know that many of you are here in a mood of challenge. Perhaps you do not really believe you can learn anything from a lecture on the appreciation of music. You have gone to concerts and fallen asleep. You were bored. Your wife was bored, too, but she had a new dress and she was determined to wear it.

But symphonic music is not as bad as it sounds. Unlike hillbilly, rock'n'roll and the twist, you have to listen creatively.

Let us take Pascanini's Symphony in D-flat, often called

The Blast from Hades. It opens with the theme stated clearly by the oboe and momentarily contradicted by the strings. (*He hums a frightening bit of disharmonious sound.*) If I were an oboe it would sound better, of course. A crash is now heard. Pascanini was uncanny here. He had the drummer deliberately throw tin cans at his cymbals to create the eerie effect of tin cans being thrown at cymbals.

This would be jarring were it not for the sudden entrance of the flute (who was a little late for dinner), announcing Beatrice's theme. It is a very sweet bit of melody signifying the innocence of Beatrice, who is later to fall down a manhole and descend into Hades seeking her boy friend, Tab, who has been changed into a black duck by the Greek god Zeus as punishment for not taking off his hat in the palace.

The music makes this very clear . . . so: (*Hums or plays ghastly passage on the phonograph*) The legend is strained a bit here, for actually, Tab was punished for parking his chariot in a no-parking zone. It does not affect the music.

At any rate, the flute tosses the theme to the strings, who pick it up for a moment and then throw it at the French horn, rather unexpectedly. The French horn distorts the theme . . . darkening it, and mixing it with turpentine and molasses, one might say, only to throw it in a wild frenzy to the trumpet, who misses it . . . and it goes for an incomplete pass—third down and twelve bars to go in the first movement.

These twelve bars are a repetition by the entire orchestra of the same chord—a flat eleventh, for those in the know—which is followed, very wisely, by about thirty

seconds of silence. Pascanini, genius that he was, knew
that the audience would all want to cough about here—
those who didn't want to rush out for some fresh air—so
he wrote in some silence.

In the second movement . . . so: (*Hums same wild
theme as before, or plays same passage on the phonograph*)
The whole thing has changed. Beatrice is down the manhole and on her way to the lower depths and the fiery pit,
while her boy friend seems to be a dead duck. This is terribly sad, and Pascanini has not neglected it. There is a
recording of the world premiere of this symphony in
which tears from the musicians splash on the drums, giving the effect of a rainstorm. Extremely wistful.

But suddenly as we reach the final movement . . . so,
(*Hums or plays the same passage*) a piccolo, a loud piccolo, announces the theme of the final movement, a movement of hope because it will soon end.

What Pascanini has done here is take Schubert's *Un-
finished Symphony,* the famous "You are my song of love"
theme, and played it upside down and backwards, thus
not only more or less finishing it for Schubert but creat-
ing an utterly new dimension in Pascanini's own symphony.
(*Plays or hums the same passage*) Notice how brightness
has crept in? How lightness appears? How the violins are
brilliant? Beatrice has found her duck and she recognizes
him by his soulful eyes. She needs only to embrace him
to cast off the wicked spell and go back up the manhole
to 14th Street and happiness ever afterward. This she
does, and the music is most telling.

So delightful does the composition become, so gay and
jolly and hopeful, that nothing but a flute plays for a
while, during which there are little knocks and bangs as

the violinists and trumpeters run around the stage filled with delight, banging each other over the head in sheer exuberance. A great roll of the kettledrums tells us that the joyful end has been reached.

There is then a brief coda ending this great work. Thus the listener is left with a lovely melodious theme . . . so: (*Hums or plays the same passage*)

Of course it sounds *much* better when you hear the whole thing. Next week I shall discuss Walter Fragment's very modern symphony featuring a plumber banging on pipes accompanied by the strings and brass. If you have ever had a sink overflow you will want to understand this great contemporary work by Walter Fragment. Just to whet your appetite I shall give you a bit of the opening of the second movement where the sink becomes stopped up. (*Hums or sings or plays same passage*)

Don't miss it.

THE END

16 | A GOOD TRICK

(Anyone can do this. All that is needed are four or five tennis balls or brightly colored rubber balls—even more, if possible. The worse the juggling is done, the better.

The juggler comes out holding a container and a number of balls. He bounces a few, and throws one up and catches it. He throws two up and misses one. He throws up several, and picks them up when they fall. He puts them all down in container.)

Ladies and gentlemen, I am prepared to juggle twelve balls, using my hands, feet and head. This is a feat only the greatest jugglers have ever attempted, and few have succeeded. After I have twelve balls going I shall revolve a delicate china plate on my nose and, holding a stick between my teeth, I shall balance there any small child in the audience who can stand still. *(Pause)* Don't mock me! There is an undercurrent of mockery pervading this audience. I come from a long line of artists. I am not here to waste time.

Laugh. Go ahead. They laughed at Columbus.

(He starts to juggle three balls without much success.)

This child I am going to balance with a stick and my teeth *must* stand still, you understand. I do not perform miracles. Everything I do can be duplicated by human means and forty-two years of practice.

As I said, they laughed at Columbus. (*Pause*) Has anyone in the audience a delicate china plate, a child who can stand still, and a solid-gold watch? While I am doing all this balancing I break a watch in pieces with one foot. I often put it back together, too.

(*Waits very briefly*) No one. Well. Let's wait a minute. As I was saying, they laughed at Columbus. He said to his mother, "Ma, I'm going to sail around the world." His mother said, "Can't you stay home *one night?*" Columbus said, "Look, Ma, somebody's got to sail around the world and find a new route to the Indies—spices, delicate spices of the Indies . . ." His mother said, "You don't like my spaghetti? Delicate spices? What's wrong with oregano? Garlic isn't delicate enough?"

That's how it went. Any time anyone comes up with something new and brilliant, like my juggling act . . . Look at James Watt. He's sitting in the kitchen making instant tea and he notices the lid is popping off the kettle. "Papa," he yells. "Papa. Guess what?" Papa says, "You want the car tonight. I know." James Watt says, "No, Papa. I just discovered steam. *Steam!*" His father shrugs. The way my public shrugs. "Steam?" says his father. "Who needs it?" James Watt is stunned. "Papa, if steam can push the top off a kettle, it can push a boat on the river. A steamboat! Steamboats on the river. Jazz coming on down to New Orleans . . . King Oliver . . . and steam horses . . ." His father gives him a belt. "O.K., dope. Quiet down and make the tea."

That's the way it is.

(*He starts juggling a number of balls hopefully. They fall all over. He apologizes.*) I have to warm up, you know. (*Pause*) If there is a small child in the audience who can stand still and hesitates to come up because of fear, I assure him, when I get going there is nothing to worry about. (*Pause*) All right, be skeptical.

The public always scoffs at everything. Look at Edison. He works night after night by candlelight and moonlight, Thomas Alva Edison. The man is working on a bulb, a vacuum bulb, a bulb that will give steady light by electricity. One night after months of work his wife says, "We never go anywhere. Every night you sit there with that *thing*. We haven't been dancing since the year we were married." She is scoffing. More months go by. Edison is dedicated. He is working for something. He wants his picture on a postage stamp, for one thing.

Once more his wife: "You don't even speak to me any more. You and your gadgets. I'll bet when it's finished it won't work, whatever it is."

More months pass. Autumn turns to winter. It always does. One day Edison jumps up and cries with joy. The darn thing *lights up*. He calls his wife. "Poopsie! Poopsie-Woopsie. I did it!" His wife comes in skeptically. She looks at it with a sneer. She goes over and bends over the first electric light. She shouts at it. "Hello? Hello? Is this you, Marge?" She waits a few moments. Nothing happens. She turns to Edison. "It doesn't work," she says, and walks out.

There you are.

(*He starts juggling everything possible. He catches a few balls, and the rest fall all over.*)

Is there . . . a young child in the audience . . . or a delicate china plate? (*Waits*)

That's what I thought. No faith.

(*Throws all the balls up in the air and walks toward exit. He stops at the edge of the stage and turns to audience.*) You know what they said to Bell when he first invented the telephone? They said, "You'll never get to use it. Your wife will be on it all the time." (*Exits*)

THE END

17 | WHAT'S WRONG
WITH THE WORLD

(This is a good example of what the trade calls a "stand-up" monologue. A stand-up monologue is addressed to the audience, although the actress may, in fact should, use as much pantomime as possible and, where it seems effective, pretend there is another person present. Monologues of this sort require a rapport with the audience, as if you were talking to friends. Be serious about it, no matter how much the audience laughs. If you are making a sound point and it provokes laughter, be even more serious and ad lib, "I mean it. Really. I'm not joking."

(This monologue should be done by a woman, in a housewifely apron, although this is not necessary. She should be plaintive rather than angry, and in talking about jar tops, pins in shirts, and so on, should use gestures to indicate the difficulties.)

What is really wrong with the world has nothing to do with the money spent on space research, or the economic system, or communism, or any of those great issues. The great issues don't drive you frantic day in and day out.

They either knock you for a loop, or the President takes care of them.

It's the nagging little things that cause trouble. Nothing is made right any more. Nothing fits right. Trains don't run on time. The program you look forward to on TV is postponed to make way for a documentary on Icelandic fishing and its importance to world economics. If you dye a rug and don't have enough dye and you go back, the same green you bought yesterday is now a shade darker. Different lot. The girl who promised to be there at noon promptly to help out for your daughter's big party can't come because she's taking part in a mass baptism or a meeting of the part-time maids' union, which is considering affiliating with the teamsters.

Furniture comes apart when a special guest sits down. Wallpaper peels off laughingly and waves at you a month after it's been glued on by a paper hanger who turns out to be a grade-school principal earning a little extra money.

It goes on and on, doesn't it?

You want your roof fixed? A couple of shingles blown up by a storm or chewed up by squirrels? A man comes and looks it over, putting his foot through the roof in several places to make the job four times as expensive. Then it rains, and he can't work in the rain. Then it turns cold, and he's afraid the nails will freeze or something. In fact he can't come until next spring. When he does finally come he breaks two windows with his extension ladder and then pounds so hard that the plaster cracks in the bedrooms. After he's finally done and you pay the bill which is twice the estimate—estimates are just for kicks— he sues you because he skinned his knuckles.

Then the TV man arrives and fixes your aerial, making

another hole in the roof. You have to have the aerial fixed because the stainless steel, guaranteed impervious to any chemical action, has rusted rotten.

Just like the lifetime chrome on your car. Have you ever noticed how gaily companies toss about the word "lifetime"? A lifetime guarantee can be anything from thirty days to a year. It's the lifetime of a mouse or a butterfly they're talking about.

Guarantees are enough to drive you crazy anyway. They always guarantee to take care of anything except what happens. And they *know* what's going to happen because even as you stand in the doorway of the shop, the man smiles and says, "I know. The steam iron is spurting water." This is not guaranteed. What is guaranteed on the steam iron is probably that the handle will not wear through.

Medical insurance works out the same way in my world. I don't know about yours. But whatever the doctor tells me has to be done—the medical policy specifically exempts it, and usually in red ink. You have to catch the diseases *they* want.

And clothes? What is wrong with the world is that clothes are sewed together with thread calculated to dissolve on contact with water—often just on contact with the human body. Ever take a real good look at the inside of a dress or coat? It looks as if the mice had chewed the seams for a week. Get the dress cleaned, or wash it, and you get it back in panels. Everything comes apart.

Buttons are worse. You take a dress home from the store and as you button the third button, your finger goes right through the hole with the button on the end—of your finger, I mean. Oh, well, is it so hard to sew on

buttons and reinforce them? Not for you. For manufac-
turers it's impossible. And suppose you lose a button. How
can you help it? A strong wind will blow them off a shortie
coat.

Ever try to match a button? They don't make them.
Nobody *ever* makes the buttons that match the ones you
need. There is an international conspiracy *not* to make
buttons that match any other buttons. All right. So what?
Buy a whole new set of buttons. Oho! When they tell you
the price of buttons you wonder if they keep them in a
guarded vault.

Now, let's be calm. If I mention stockings, will everybody promise not to panic? Good. I know how you feel.
They tell you to buy two pair of stockings at once because
if one goes you have three left. Is that right? Maybe you're
supposed to put *two* on the *cold* leg. Anyway, the idea is
that your stockings are going to run fast so you ought to
have plenty. I see, now. If one goes, you use the other, and
then when that goes, you use the other. It's like having
four pair, I've heard. To me it's like having no pair.

You go home and pull on the stockings carefully, being
cautious of hangnails—in fact, it's best to get a manicure.
You get them up *so* slowly and gently . . . aah . . . that
wasn't the shade the girl showed you, but they're stockings
and they're on with no casualties. Of course you've got to
put on your shoes now. You've got to bend over to put on
your shoes. Wham! Pop! There's a run. (*Pause and sigh*)

You know that old stockings or stockings with runs are
very good to wrap up things with? Old magazines, bunches
of shirts, and the necks of the people who made the stockings. In the latter case make a good, tight knot. It might
run.

How about around the kitchen? The magnetic can-opener that drops the stewed tomatoes upside down on your shoes? Handy gadget. Product of know-how. Know-how to sell, that is. Not know-how to make.

The lovely knife sharpener that makes a saw out of your carving knife. The stainless steel flatware that turns gray. The china coffee cups that turn brown. The milk that turns blue. Or is blue to start with. I'll bet you never saw a blue cow . . . and yet, and yet . . . Finally the little odds and ends. Free-flowing salt that nothing can prevent from coming out except the slightest humidity in the air. Improved ketchup bottles that no ketchup comes out of until you bang them, and then you get a bowl of thick tomato soup running down your arms. Whipped cream pressure cans. You just shake them and thick, luscious, imitation whipped cream squirts all over the wallpaper.

Pickle jars with the easy-to-get-off tops. Simply take three different kinds of can openers, twisters, pliers and see if you can beat the talent of the machine that screwed that top on. Bang the top on the kitchen sink. Run scalding water on it. Finally dig holes with an ice pick and try to pry the lid off with a cold chisel.

I could go on forever. Hi-fi records that are low-fi. Indestructible toys that break on the way home. Gray rinses that leave your hair purple. Raspberry jam made with apples. Local corn that comes wilted from five hundred miles away. (Small world, isn't it?) Water-resistant watches that stop in a heavy fog. Self-addressed envelopes companies send you to mail their bills in. The bill won't fit in the envelope. Giant-sized quarts. Are they bigger than the small-sized quarts? Quarts? What am I saying? There are no more quarts. There are just quarter-gallons. Pound packages of raisins with fifteen ounces in them. Waterproof coats that get soaked and wet you to your skin.

Well, what's the use? We can all face the vital issues. We can stand up with courage and fellowship against war and poverty and fear. It's the ice cream made with powdered milk and genuine imitation strawberry that is going to wear us out eventually, or the Ripe Red lipstick that comes out orange, or the easily-assembled, Jim Dandy, knocked-down stainless coffee table that has been knocked down for three years around my house waiting for a graduate engineer or a master cabinet-maker to put it together: These are the things that will be to blame if Western civilization perishes. A nation whose engineering genius cannot make a stocking that will not run, cannot long endure.

THE END

18 THE GREAT SINGER

(A serious-looking man or woman is seated onstage, holding a pad and pencil. He gets up to greet a visitor, smiles, and shakes hands.)

Welcome to Torts University, Mr. Rock Pyle. Please sit down. Mr. Pyle, as chairman of the Folk Song Division of our Department of Primitive People, I feel it is a great honor to have you here for an interview with me. I know you have a busy schedule, having just sung some of your stirring songs at the Municipal Auditorium, and going on to another show tonight, so I'll try to make our talk brief.

As I told you in my letter, we in the Department of Primitive People are studying modern rock and roll from a standpoint of sociology, anthropology, and elementary harmony. We feel that your type of singing compares with the weird chants of the African native as well as the screams and wails of the voodoo cults of Haiti. All through history men have made songs of simple folk material, from the Tongus of Siberia singing across the tundra to their reindeer, "Ooooh! koo-a-koo, boo. Hey! koo-aboo-boo," to the Indians at the tip of South America stomping out their wedding song, "Unga unga, ooooh wadda boo-boo, *wadda boo-boo!*"

What I want to get is the authentic feel of a great singer of the people like you, a humble boy who is yet a hero to the American people. I want to get the low-down feel of the beat of your great music.

First, though, Mr. Pyle, some biographical material. Oh, by the way, I notice your clothing is all torn and you're barefoot. Also, there are no strings on your guitar . . . or should I say, ha ha, *gee*tar? Ahem. . . . What's that? Your loyal fans tore your clothes for souvenirs? How touching. . . . Took your shoes, too? And the guitar strings? . . . Oh, you can't play it, anyway. . . . What's that? Yes, I notice most of your competitors play only one chord, anyway. I think it's very progressive of you to move ahead to playing *no* chords.

Now, where were you discovered and by whom, Mr. Pyle? (*Listens carefully*) Three years ago, on July 12th, by Sol Winkleman, while singing to the pigs back in Melissa, Mississippi. You sprung directly from the earth, one might say. Very fundamental.

Now, what was Mr. Winkleman's impression? I assume he was a lover of folk and primitive music as I am, and a deep student of rituals. . . . He did, eh? Said you were a natural-born singer like Caruso and Presley. . . . You were calling to the cows at the time? Oh, the sows. Yes, I know. Soweeee! Lovely sound.

Can you remember your first record, the one that sold five million copies? How is that again? A little more slowly please, Mr. Pyle. (*Recites slowly, as if repeating*)

I once had a lovely sow,
But I ain't got it now.

Traded it for a lonesome cow.
Traded it for a bad old cow.
Traded it for a sad old cow.
Didn't want any cow
Any how.
I wish now,
I had me back my lovely sow.

Truly a gigantic conception, Mr. Pyle. It has deep, sub-conscious connotations. It speaks of the beginning of the earth when man walked alone. Yes.

Now, what is your ambition, Mr. Pyle? Would you like to be in motion pictures or on the stage? . . . I see. Uh-huh. You've been offered the parts of King Lear, George Washington and Romeo, but you believe you belong to the people. I agree, Mr. Pyle. I look on you as a sort of rocking George Washington, an Abe Lincoln with a beat.

Now, Mr. Pyle, it seems to me that to understand you and your simple but profound music, music that stirs the heart and feet of every adolescent in the country—I beg pardon? Yes, that is correct—in the *world,* you must have some message for the young people of America? . . . Not so quickly, Mr. Pyle. That charming southern accent is a little difficult for Northern ears, ha ha. (*Pause*)

You believe they should live a good, clean life, obeying their parents and keeping their hot rods down to fifty miles an hour. Now what about morals? Eh? . . . You think they should definitely have them. How simply put, and how true.

Now, Mr. Pyle, I believe the basic part of your work is the beat. That is, your rhythmic motion with shoulders, feet, head and so forth. This is the primitive soul in you expressing itself. (*The professor stands up and appears to be watching.*)

How do you manage these effects? Beg pardon? . . . I see. You just open your mouth and let your deep emotions take over. . . . You just what? You just "get with it." I see. Is it difficult to . . . uh . . . get with it? Pardon? Oh, you have to be hip. One could learn to be hip, I imagine— one could acquire the ability to get with it, man. Could you show me how you manage a few elementary motions? (*The professor watches and then mimics.*)

I see. Stamp left foot. Oh, twice. Stamp right foot. Shake knees together. Yes, I follow you. Oh, twice. Yes. Revolve shoulders as needed. Throw back head for loud parts. This is fascinating.

I happen to have a folk song from the Cajun area of Louisiana I'd like to try. I mean, it would help me immeasurably to get inside this rhythmic phenomenon. Could I borrow your guitar? *Gee*-tar. Yes, only a square would say guitar. Ah ha ha. Let me see now. (*He sings to the following words. Any melody will do. The more elementary and monotonous it is, the better. The more exaggerated the stomping and the enthusiasm, the better, too. The professor starts off simply, almost like a delicate folk singer, but by the third line or so he is really "with it."*)

"Oh, Mammy, make those pickles that I love,
(*He stamps twice, rolls his shoulders.*)
Those sweet and juicy pickles that I love.
(*Stamps, rolls, throws back head.*)
Oh, Mammy, cook those pickles, make them hot,
Those silly, dilly pickles in your pot.
(*He stamps his feet, rolls his shoulders and shouts.*)

Rock on down, man! Yah!
I have tasted others cookin'
But you don't give them a look in.
Saints above!
With your pickled piccalilli—
Gosh, it drives me silly.
That pickled piccalilli that I love!
Hey, ree de bop!
That pickled piccalilli that I love."

(*He stops, radiantly happy and almost exhausted.*) What's that? . . . Oh, that's very kind, coming from a great artist like you. I do believe I'll demonstrate this at the next meeting of the Society of Folk and Primitive Singing and Dancing. (*He starts again.*)

"With your pickled piccalilli—
Gosh, it drives me silly.
That pickled piccalilli that I love! . . ."

(*Exits, singing wildly*)

THE END

19 | GIVE TILL IT HURTS

(Mrs. Laidlaw, *a young married woman, has the chore of raising some money by telephone solicitation. There are a telephone, a chair and a book onstage. She looks in her book thoughtfully, flipping pages, then dials a number on the telephone.*)

Hello? Hello, John? How's my darling husband this morning? What, dear? Oh. You *know* anchovies and you don't get along. I *am* sorry. Look, dear, let's not fight. I need advice. Darling, I don't know everything. Darling, this is vital. What? No, I'm not buying anything. I'm home.

Look, Poopsie . . . what? Well, people shouldn't *be* on your line. Dear, I have to solicit funds for the PTA, and I took a book out of the library telling all the best approaches. Oh, you're so funny, darling. No, it doesn't say anything about a gun in anybody's back. Ha ha. Be serious. You are? Hmn.

No, I'm not caught up in any flim-flam. The school— Junior's grade three, I should say—needs to be modernized. They have one picture, for example . . . (*Pause*) Calvin Coolidge. Uh? I know there's nothing wrong with

Calvin Coolidge. But it would be nice to have a newer President. Then the inkwells—they're so crusted with old ink you can hardly get any new ink in them. And the blackboard squeaks? Grease what? Grease the chalk? Darling, you are *not* being very helpful.

We need two hundred dollars to start. That's our goal. No, you can't sell two hundred dollars' worth of brownies! Everybody in the PTA is on a diet. Besides, the last time we sold fifty dollars' worth of brownies they cost us sixty. All right, dear, I know you're busy. I thought you'd be interested in your own child's education.

What? I'm sure I can raise the money. I know I can raise it. All right. Goodbye. (*Pauses and sighs*)

Men!

(*Looks through book*) Neighborly approach. Hmn. (*Dials phone*) Hello? Hello, Mrs. Skiffington? This is Marge Laidlaw, your friendly neighbor. What? Well, everybody who says she's your friendly neighbor isn't selling insurance or brushes. . . . No, or giving free cha-cha lessons either. Mrs. Skiffington, as a friendly neighbor you must know how badly grade three at Beechwood Grade School needs help. . . . Beg pardon? Well, Mrs. Skiffington, giving to the Society for the Prevention of Cruelty to Animals is one thing, very admirable, too, but those children with clogged inkwells and squeaky blackboards . . . Mrs. Skiffington! Dear, neighborly Mrs. . . . (*Pause*) She hung up. Wait till she wants to borrow my portable TV again!

(*She goes through her book again.*) Confident approach that assumes the party contacted will give. I'll just try that on Mrs. Reed. (*She dials and speaks with crisp assurance.*)

Hello. This is Marge Laidlaw of the Beechwood PTA, vice-president in charge of donations. I am sure, Mrs. Reed,

that I can put you down for twenty dollars toward modern-
izing. . . . What was that? How many books do I have?
What Green Stamps? I don't have any books. I save the
plaid ones, anyway. Besides, I never *do* get to paste them in.
Ten thousand for a school bus? No, thank you. We have
a bus. (*Hangs up*) Wrong number. (*Dials again*)

I don't know what we're coming to! Hello? Minnie
Reed? Marge Laidlaw here. Beechwood PTA. Shall I put
you down for ten or twenty? No, *dollars*. We don't need
doughnuts. Minnie, it's to modernize Grade Three. Well,
just a start. Maybe sweep up the fallen plaster. Then we
need new seats. A new picture of a President. That's kind
of you, but *Washington Crossing the Delaware* wasn't
what we had in mind. . . . Minnie, we had a dance last
year, and we had to borrow from the revolving fund to pay
for the refreshments. We went into the red. I know it
was fun, but. . . . Eh? Bingo is against the law in this
state? I know you're trying to be helpful, but what we
need is money, not advice. What? Someone at the door?
That's a pretty old gag, Minnie. That one and the one
about the dinner burning. Minnie! (*Hangs up*)

She didn't have to hang up. I wasn't through. (*Pause*)
Or was I? (*Pause. Glances through book*) There must be
some successful approach. Hmn. Patriotic. The flag. O'er
the ramparts we watch. America the Beautiful. Yes. (*Dials
a number. Waits for a moment*)

Hello, Mrs. Thomas? Marge Laidlaw here. Really? Oh,
I *am* sorry. It does seem an odd time of day to be taking
a shower. (*Pause*) Well, you're out of the shower now.
Why bring up old problems? I'm sure you won't mind
talking a moment. Mrs. Thomas, I have always known
you to be a loyal American, proud of the nation we have

built. No doubt you come from pioneer stock, people who fought at Bunker Hill . . . What? Well, what does it matter what side they were on? Your ancestors were there, weren't they? That's what counts, I always say. The flag flying proudly in the breeze on the Fourth of July. . . . (*She refers hastily to her book*) must send a cold shiver of patriotism down your spine. Up *and* down. Mrs. Thomas, as a woman who loves her country, from the rock-ribbed coast of Maine to the fogbound shores of . . . I mean, *sunlit* shores of California, you must understand that love of country starts in the first years of school, when we learn about George Washington, Abraham Lincoln, Betsy Ross, Fanny Farmer, and . . . What? I'm so sorry. Yes, it *is* a cold day to be standing there in a skimpy towel, dripping. Yes . . . Yes . . . I know . . . (*Sharply*) Well, how was I to know you were taking a shower?

(*She hangs up, and looks through the book again, wearily. She thinks for a moment, then dials.*) The desperate approach. Well, might as well try it. Heaven knows I *am* desperate.

(*Into phone*) Hello, Amy Tuttle? Marge Laidlaw here. Amy, I am desperate. What? I haven't called you in weeks? Amy, I've been busy. My husband had hives and Junior took a watch apart. Oh, all sorts of troubles piling up. Amy, I wouldn't pass you by on the street with my nose in the air. I must have been thinking of something. Amy, please. I need help. When I think of those poor, neglected children in Grade Three, trying to write from clogged inkwells, staring silently at Calvin Coolidge and fallen plaster. . . . Amy, hear me out. My need is great. Open your heart, Amy. I have to get two hundred dollars for

the PTA Modernization Fund and I haven't a nickel yet.
. . . Amy, I did *not* see you. I would not snub you. Amy,
please, I need . . . Beg pardon? What ten dollars I owe
you? Oh? Hmn. Oh, yes, when I bought the little felt hat
and didn't have my wallet. Amy, it was not six months
ago. All right, Amy, just forget I called you. I'll see you
around the bridge club. Goodbye, Amy. (*Hangs up*)

I had forgotten all about that ten dollars. (*Looks
through book once more*) Hmn. Gentle approach. Soft
sell. I'm in no mood to be gentle, but here goes.

(*Dials. Waits. Speaks sweetly and affectionately*) Hello,
Kay? Marge Laidlaw. Look, Kay . . . Sure we got home
all right. My husband? He's fine. Look, Katie . . . Your
daughter? 97 in spelling and captain of the field hockey
team? Isn't that the loveliest thing. Look, Katherine, dear
. . . Beg pardon? He did? All by himself? Wonderful. All
the way to his violin lesson, crossing streets and everything by himself, for the first time. That boy of yours is
really growing up. He what? . . . He lost his violin on
the way? Well, as long as he took an important step by
himself, that's what counts. Look, Kay . . . Oh, really?
No, I haven't had time. I've been working for the PTA.
There's this drive for (*She says this very rapidly, almost
incoherently.*) funds-to-modernize-grade-three-and-we-are-
asking-for-contributions-from . . . (*Takes a deep breath*)
Your brother what? Engaged to Dorothy Farnum. The
Pittsfield Farnums. No, the ones I know live in Brookline.
Eh? Well, they haven't much choice. The place was willed
to them. Yes, I've heard of the Pittsfield Farnums. Oh,
how nice! A party to celebrate—but you what? Oh, your
liver. Hmn. Spots in front of your eyes. Hmn. Uh-huh

. . . uh-huh . . . uh-huh . . . Yes . . . no . . . uh-huh
. . . uh-huh . . . (*Listens sadly and impatiently, inter-jecting little uh-huhs. She opens her mouth to speak now and then, but shuts it wearily. Finally she gets to say something.*)

Uh-huh . . . Doctor says unusual case. Yes, well, they can be a lot of trouble. Hmn, expensive, too. Yes, well, nice to have talked to you, Kay. 'Bye now, I've got a roast in the oven that I think is burning, and somebody's at the front door. The bell is ringing madly. 'Bye. (*Hangs up and groans. Suddenly*) That was the limit!

(*She looks through the book again, leafing over pages without interest. Finally she flings the book aside and dials. She speaks cooingly.*) Hello, John? This is your little loving wifey. How is your poor tummy? That's good. Look, Poopsie . . . all right, dear . . . look, John, you know that mink stole you were going to get me for my birthday? What, darling? . . . Yes, you were. I know you got me a bracelet for my birthday last month. I'm talking about my next birthday. Well, I sort of charged it, darling. Just in anticipation. It's only four hundred dollars. . . . What, angel? Four hundred dollars is cheap for a mink stole. Darling, it was a steal. The stole was a steal. Oh, ha ha ha! I saved you two hundred dollars easily. . . . What, dear? Where is it? The two hundred I saved you? Darling, you *have* it. You're not going to have to spend it, you see? So I thought if you could write me a check for the two hundred so we could modernize the third grade. . . . What, dear? You don't think that's much of a saving? I see. By the way, angel, they have this other mink stole for a thousand dollars that's simply glorious, and . . . What, dear? Forget it, you'll write the check? Oh, John, I *knew* you'd understand. . . . Yes, darling. I'll tell the girls. Goodbye, precious. Steak for dinner tonight! 'Bye.

(*Hangs up and smiles triumphantly*) He's *so* thoughtful. And Betsy and Joan both said I'd never be able to collect it. They just don't *know* my knack for this sort of thing.

THE END

20 | BE YOURSELF

(This little act is done by a man. It would be nice to have a full-length mirror available, but it is not necessary. At any rate, as he goes on he poses before a mirror—real or imaginary—turning away now and then. He is really talking out loud to himself, of course. Let's call him Jerry Jones.

Jerry *stares into the mirror, turns his face to one side, rubs his chin and holds his head high. He looks at his profile, but finds it hard to see his profile without looking out of the corner of his eye. He throws his shoulders back and looks again. Then he smiles with sickening charm, frowns coldly, and sighs.)*

What do you act like when you ask the most beautiful girl in the whole entire university—Miss Snowflake of the Winter Carnival, no less—to the prom, and she says *yes?* Gee, she hardly knows me . . . I mean the *real* me, the me that's inside, down deep . . . the me that people don't dig. Fact is, nobody really knows me—they just see the surface, the shell.

Trouble is, there are so many real me's that it's hard

to know which one to be for the most beautiful girl in the University. If I only knew how *she* would want me to be, I'd be it. I have all *sorts* of possibilities. The vocational counselor at school said I could be almost anything. It's up to me. I am the master of my fate, the captain of my soul, and the manager of the tennis team.

Gosh! Lovely, beautiful, talented Kim Johnson—a whole evening with her. She's so gorgeous. How do you act with a gorgeous girl? I know how to act with dogs. I know how to act with the run-of-the-mill chick. I don't know why she agreed to come with me anyway. Maybe she *likes* me. I guess she must. But what me does she like? It can't be the real me, because that's buried deep.

I guess they all like the he-man type. (*He poses before the mirror, acting like a he-man football hero.*) "Yes, Kim, just let any of those mugs say a word out of place and I'll break every bone in their bodies." (*He mimics breaking bones in various bodies.*) "What? Kim? What's six touchdowns against Army? Is Army so hot? Ha ha. Yes, I played both offense and defense. Played all the way. Iron Man Jerry Jones, they call me."

(*Suddenly deflates like a balloon*) I'm no iron man. That's not me. She knows darn well I'm a third-string tackle anyway. They send the manager in before me. A plague would have to sweep the bench before *I* got in.

I could be the egghead. The REAL me has a lot of the egghead in him. I really *am* a brain if I put my mind to it. Sometimes I feel very intellectual. I mean, like when I read *The Catcher in the Rye* twice. And *War and Peace,* almost. (*Goes to mirror and becomes cool intellectual*)

"Kim, my dear, the possibilities of economic entanglement with the European Common Market are enormous.

The output of ingots will exceed the outgo of inputs for sure. Yes. Well, I wouldn't say James Joyce's *Ulysses* is *exactly* the peak of literary accomplishment in English. We must remember there is a certain incoherence . . . in spite of the impressionism. Kazin says that Joyce. . . . Wagner? Well, his music is not as bad as it sounds, as they say. (*Pause*) Oh, I'm no wit, Kim. Not really. I just say things with terse appropriatenessity . . . ness . . . ness-ness . . ." (*Turns away*) Oh, heck. I'll never be cool. Not really *cool*. I don't even dig Brubeck. In fact, I even like Dixieland. Not that I'd tell. And I think Bach stinks, I don't care how cool he is. He isn't cool, he's *dead*.

Maybe the poetic approach. The real me is probably a poet. My English teacher says I could be another Byron if I really gave it the old try. (*Goes to mirror. Mimics slightly delicate, wistful poet*) "Kim, Kim, star of the purple twilight, song that sings in the night with muffled violins and muted trumpets. Kim, your very name is a . . . a . . . well, I'll think of something . . . a melody . . . supreme. Your lips are the autumn's scarlet glory, the promised kiss of springtime. Shall I compare thee to a summer's day? Kim, the name rings out like sharp temple bells in far Kashmir. Dancing here with you and your lips . . . rosebuds on fire—let's sit this one out. Love is burning my breast . . . chest. . . ." (*Turns away, disgusted*)

I can't make it that way. I'd forget my lines. I'd just look at her and tremble and grin and dance and hold my face a little against hers and smell her perfume and be in Heaven, but would I *impress* her? She is the most sought-after girl in school. I can't just say, "Gee, you're nice," and hope to have her forever and ever come rain or come shine, day in day out and all that jazz. Which is the ultimate object, isn't it? I mean the truth must lie somewhere in the real me.

I could be humble. I *am* humble. Essentially the real me, down deep . . . the me I have to bring up . . . essentially it is humble. (*Looks in mirror. Tries to look humble and adoring*) "Kim, I am nothing compared to you. You are a star in Heaven and I am worthless dust. It's only your magic, your radiance, that makes me anything. With my humility and your wonder—*man!* Kim, how you can see anything in me is beyond my comprehension." No . . . no . . . No! (*Stops, agitated and worn out. Moves away from mirror*)

Oh, the heck with it. I'll just be me. Just plain Jerry Jones, manager of the tennis team, third-string tackle, a lazy C-student who'll end up a second vice-president in the largest thumb-tack factory west of the Mississippi. That's probably the real me. When I ever get to dig down deep and find the real me, that's what I'll probably find.

Maybe the real *she* is just shy and scared like the real me! *Man,* that's a possibility. How about that? Suppose the real *she* is as shy as the real me, and we just didn't fake or kid and our eyes just met and we understood. (*Long, honest, hopeful sigh*)

Boy! I'm going to find out. (*Runs off stage*)

THE END

21 | GOD REST YE MERRY, GENTLEMEN

(This had best be done by a woman. She is putting up and trimming a large Christmas tree while her husband, George, helps. I don't know why husbands are so often named George, but they are, and we have to live with it. No props are necessary, but it would be nice to have a little artificial snow or icicles and similar decorations.)

George, hold it up. Get behind it and hold it straight. If there's anything I cannot bear it's a crooked Christmas tree. Junior, get out from behind. What? Daddy doesn't need anybody to hold his cigar. He's not going to need his nasty cigar. Junior! You're pulling it over! Junior, do you know what Santa Claus is going to do? He's going to go right over this house. . . . What? Oh, you spoke to him at Johnson's, confidentially, alone? You told him what? . . . I hollered at you all the time? Junior, it is poor taste to tell things like that to Santa Claus. Junior, get out of there. Go put bulbs in the light thing, or take a bath or something. Of course you have to take a bath Christmas week.

George, get behind it . . . hold it straight. I'll only
be a minute. I've been decorating trees since I was eleven.
. . . What? It's not *that* long ago. That isn't the Yuletide
spirit. Junior, stop bouncing those bulbs. They don't
bounce. Junior, if Santa Claus took you up on the chim-
ney and let a reindeer kick you, I wouldn't be surprised.
Now sit down and be quiet.

All right, hold it steady, George. We'll just toss some
icicles here and some snow here . . . drape some tinsel
here and some red rope and green rope. (*Stands back.
Moves farther back and observes carefully*)

Are you sure you've wired that steady now, George?
Well, it tilts a bit, but we can fix that later. A green and
blue ball here, some long red ones here . . . (*She pretends to drop and attach decorations while she giddily
sings "God Rest Ye Merry, Gentlemen" and "Oh, Christmas Tree," etc. Finally she stands back to look.*) There!
That's nice and even and gay. Isn't it, George? George!
Where are you, George? *George!* (*Waits a moment. Looks
around the room*) Stop giggling, Junior. He's where? . . .
Behind the tree. (*She goes around.*)

Come out, George. Why didn't you speak up? . . . You
had your mouth stuffed with tinsel? Did I do that? . . .
I'm sorry. But you could have come out, couldn't you?
You what? . . . You wired yourself to the tree? George,
that wasn't very thoughtful. You can't just *stand* there for
the Twelve Days of Christmas. Here, let me cut the wire.

Junior! Stop laughing. What? . . . It is not a bit like
cowboys and Indians on TV. Your father accidentally tied
himself to the tree. A tree is something important—it's
symbolic. It's nothing to laugh at. You all right now,
George? (*She laughs herself.*) I'm sorry. But you *do* look

odd with that red bauble dangling from your ear and the icicles in your hair and the snow on your mustache.

Come back here and look. Tell me how you like it. Back here. (*She backs away.*) It what? Needs a star up there? George, I don't think so. You what? . . . Just hold it up. We-e-ell. (*Pause*) Yes, I guess . . . (*Screams*) George! It's falling! Oh, George, why did you! George. (*Pause*) Get up from under that tree carefully. It's a mess. Simply a mess.

George, a few bruises won't hurt you, but the tree is a positive *mess*.

(*Starts to cry*) I can't bear it. I'm going to spend Christmas with my mother. That's what I'm going to do. She doesn't have a tree. She just trims her rubber plant!

THE END

22 | I PAINT WHAT I FEEL

(*This takes place in an artist's studio. An arty-looking man enters, and gesticulates wildly as he responds to his interviewer's questions.*)

Yes, I am Percival Wildman, the abstract artist. Sit down. You're from *Time Today*, the news magazine. Very perceptive journal. Yes. They said in a review of my work that my later paintings looked as if I had sat on them while they were wet. That's exactly what I did do, old chap. I want my whole personality in my art. (*Pause. He gasps.*) I'm so sorry. That's not a chair. Yes, really quite pointed and sharp. It's a portrait of my grandmother in steel and dented aluminum spoons. One of my rare pieces of sculpture. . . . Yes, that *is* a chair. Oh, go right ahead and sit on the painting. That's how I get some of my most charming effects. Having strangers sit on them gives everything an element of surprise. (*Pause*)

I beg your pardon? When did I start? I really believe that when I was in my highchair and began throwing cereal all over the place, including on my head, I began to get the feeling for abstract art. I mean, it flowed. Does anything flow better than strained bananas and cream of wheat? It has texture and personality.

Of course, as I grew older I saw suggestions of abstract art everywhere. I recall my mother seeing the work I had done on the living room walls with lipstick and a bottle of ketchup. (*He illustrates by scrawling imaginary whorls in the air.*) Oh, it was a tremendous project. My mother took one look at the wall and hit me on the head. "That'll teach you!" she said. And it did. That is, the blow was so severe that it gave me a new outlook.

In grade school I did what I called a living mural by throwing soft tomatoes and eggs at the teacher, who ducked. The patterns formed by the splatter of living matter on the blackboard exhilarated me. Then when I was in junior high school I used to love to plunge my face into a custard pie, regarding the imprint it made with rapture. As a youth I always delighted in squirting red ink in a policeman's face, for example. Oh, I've suffered for my art! Or green ink down my grandmother's neck. Or purple ink in my father's ear, watching it drip down his shirt and form astonishing patterns.

Naturally when I grew older I went to art school. I shall never forget the expression on my teacher's face when he saw me painting with a water pistol—several water pistols, I should say. I used to squirt different paints on the canvas, jumping up and down with excitement. (*He jumps up and down, squirting imaginary water pistols.*) I was expelled, of course. Everybody used to get covered with paint. They were all real fuddy-duddies, anyway, you know. I was thrown on my own. Little by little I learned how to paint physically. I mean, how to *throw* myself into it.

(*Moves around to show paintings*) Now, you take this great work, "The Edge of Hades." Notice the crisscross pattern I obtained by taking the wet canvas out in the street and letting cars and trucks run over it.

Now, this one over here, "The Moon Is a Too-Quickly-Fried Egg in January," has a great deal of me in it. I saved my hair from a haircut and worked it in. You will notice some old eggshells serene in a bed of hardened mustard. Embedded in the thick blue paint is a button that came off my shirt, and I tossed it there so I wouldn't lose it. Above, in the magenta, is an old toothbrush. The blue handle seemed superbly right.

Then over here you will notice a fairly realistic canvas showing a man's neck and shoulders, in necktie, shirt, and so forth. People say I have no sense of realism at all. I did this to prove I have. Observe that there is a hole where the head should be. At exhibitions I usually stick my own head in the hole and stay there for hours. The realism is just startling.

Finally, we have my latest work, that I am thinking of selling to the modern wing of the Metropolitan Museum. I'm not sure they're thinking of buying. But I'm thinking of selling. This is called "The Unicorn Became Extinct Because He Never Was!" I like poetic titles. It was done in collaboration with many horses at the Belmont race track. The canvas was covered with thick blotches of red, blue, green and chartreuse, and laid down on the track. For eight races the horses galloped over it, leaving delicious hoofprints that were later toned down by my sleeping on the moist painting. (*Pause*)

I beg your pardon? . . . Yes, I know you newspapermen are busy, but would you kindly remain while I do a quick painting for you? Would you like to sit on it or rub your face in it so you could say you collaborated? . . . No? I see you are a modest man.

(*He turns his back to the interviewer and starts working on a large imaginary canvas. He flings paint at it with venom. He pretends to scoop up a ball of paint and, winding up, delivers it the way a pitcher would throw to a batter. He looks for a signal from the catcher and throws another. Then he takes off one shoe and sock and pushes a bare foot against the canvas. He squares away like a prizefighter and starts boxing the painting, using his thumb and finger, now and then, to scrape paint upward and let it drip down on the painting. The next step is to butt it with his head, crying "Baa!" fiercely. Finally, pretends to set it down on the floor, takes off the other shoe and sock and does a cha-cha or twist over the painting. After a while he looks around to find the interviewer gone.*) He's gone. Well, dear, dear. I suppose great art upsets some people. (*He hops up and down looking toward the painting, then he cocks his head to one side and the other.*) I think if I went over it with an eggbeater, I might have something for the Museum of Modern Art.

THE END

23 | NEW BABY

(This little monologue is supposed to show what a young baby goes through and what he thinks about. Anyone can do it.)

Have you ever watched a new baby, say one about a month old, and wondered if there were thoughts going through his dear head as he tried to move his tiny legs and arms and made gurgling noises? I believe a new baby knows perfectly well what's going on. He hasn't learned to talk, but I rather believe this is how his thoughts go:

Well, I put one over on them that time. They went downstairs on tiptoe and thought I'd just clam up and go off to the Land of Nod for hours. I hate to be mean, but there's no sense in letting parents get the upper hand. Make them toe the mark, I say. So, just as they went downstairs to relax I let out one heck of a yowl, and they came running. Examined me all over. They knew I wasn't hungry. They couldn't find a thing wrong, of course. Ha ha. Big mystery. I bet they never thought I'd cry just for the heck of it! Boy!

If they think they can work me by Dr. Spock's book

or anybody else's book, they have another think coming. I have no intention of letting myself be neglected. After all, I don't have much fun. In a couple of weeks or so I'll be able to see my toes . . . and then I'll even put them in my mouth. Big deal. You have to do it, though. Parents expect it.

What I hate most, outside of that bath, is the way they look in the book and see when I'm supposed to hold up my head and when I'm supposed to put my foot in my mouth. I'll put my foot in my mouth when I get darn good and ready and not till then.

But that bath! They take all your clothes off and tickle you. Great fun. And that water is never warm enough. Then they tell you what a big strong man you are and how smart you are. Smart! I can't even *talk*. If I could, they'd have a different outlook, believe me.

And that father of mine! Oh, brother. He picks me up as if I were made of china. Then he pinches my thighs and says I'm going to be a football player. I have news for him. I'm going to be lazy like my grandfather Robert. He has all the fun.

Oh, brother, here comes the solid food. I heard them talking about it yesterday. They were going to try me on some kind of barley mush and squashed bananas. It sounds appalling, but I'm pretty defenseless. I can drool a little and mess up my bib, but I'm fighting a losing game. They'll take that horrible silver spoon Grandma Stelle gave them and just push the stuff down. Oh, man, when I can talk, will I explain a few things!

Here it comes. I think I'll let out a good yowl. (*Lets out a yowl, cries, thrashes about, and ends with a baby sound*)

Uggle-Buggle-uggle-*Glub*.

How about that? They thought I was talking. My old man said it was, "Hello, Daddy" and my mother explained it was, "Me hungry." All it was was simple Uggle-buggle-uggle-*Glub*. Accent on the *glub*. I like *glub*—it has a satisfying, mushy sound. I sure would never say "Me hungry." It's not even correct English.

Wow! It's coming closer. Smells like nail polish. I think I'll just reject it a few times. Don't want to give them any ideas. They'll neglect me and go skiing or play tennis if I make them feel too secure.

There! I knew it. Two minutes of goo-goo baby talk and then they get mad and stuff it down. I don't mind that barley mush but the bananas they can keep. Why not apricots or peaches? I *like* apricots. The banana growers must have a big lobby somewhere.

Now comes the burping. Talk about foggy thinking! They don't have to burp me. When I need to burp, I'll burp. In fact, when I need to do *anything* I'll do it. Make no mistake. Let's get it good and clear. A baby would never survive in today's scientific world if he let his parents run the show.

Oh-oh, here's Grandma. She's O.K., but she ought to realize I'm my mother's child and not hers. She always wants to show me to somebody, as if I were some kind of freak. I know what I look like. No hair, bent legs, button nose. I'm no movie star, I'm just a baby like any other baby, and I don't want Grandma giving me delusions of grandeur. I'll just let out a good, spine-chilling yell and she'll leave me alone. (*Lets out a spine-chilling yell, narrows down to a weird whining and up again to a good yowling. Stops suddenly*)

It hurts her feelings. But at least she leaves me alone. I'll have to learn to restrain myself a little. The way things are, I may need her help going through Yale. Financially, I mean. Boy, did I cost a lot! Well, I'm worth it, I'd say.

Oh, now it's sing-song time. Listen to this—off-key, too . . . "Oh, little Timmie, you precious angel. It's time I took you upstairs. You are ready for sleep, little precious big strong Timmie."

I have news for you. I'm not the least bit sleepy. I'm supposed to be ready to drop off for hours after a big feeding like that, but I feel wide awake.

All right, up we go, but I warn you—don't get set for four hours of peace and quiet, because I'm not the least bit sleepy. O.K. so my eyes are closing. You want me to keep them open all the time? I know I'm yawning. I like to yawn. It's one of my few hobbies. Doesn't mean a thing.

O.K. I'll go along and get in beddie-bye, but you're in for a surprise.

Nice soft bed, at that. . . . I'll just shut my eyes and pretend I'm sound asleep. Look at them tiptoe out. They hope. They're so cute, at that. I guess I ought to cooperate a little. I'll wait until they get downstairs and just give a few yowls to make sure they still love me. (*Pauses for a moment, then lets out an ear-splitting yell*)

I may be destined for opera, the way I'm developing those high notes. . . . Ah, here they come running— aren't they cute! Pick me up and make a fuss. *Pick me up.* I warn you, I don't care what the book says—I'm my own man, and no Spock is going to tell *me* how to live.

Thank you. You know what's good for you. O.K., I'll make a deal. Don't bring any strangers in here to put their cold hands on my belly and I'll sleep a while. Not long, but a while.

There they go, on tiptoe again, hopefully as ever. I guess maybe I *am* a problem; the first one always is. The second one they get wise to. I'm lucky.

Well, I *am* a little sleepy. Maybe I'll doze off a minute and then . . . (*Yawns*) I'll . . . think of . . . (*Yawns loudly*) something. (*Mutters and mumbles. Shuts eyes and smiles serenely*)

THE END

24 | WHAT'S WRONG WITH GIRLS

(This monologue is for a young man, and takes place in a restaurant. He needs a chair and, if possible, a small table before the chair. He looks at his watch three or four times impatiently. Then he pantomimes picking up a menu and looking at it, apparently becoming startled at the prices. He puts it down and looks at his watch again. At length he smiles crookedly and stands up to greet his date.)

Gee, Shirley, half-past six is not eight o'clock. I mean, there's a slight difference, especially when I'm hungry. . . . You what? You had to help your mother fix her hair? How long is her hair that it took you two hours to fix? *(He sits down.)* Shirley, I don't mind a girl being late when she isn't going steady. But when she's going steady and practically pinned she could be on time. So let her mother's hair fall down. A girl has her own life to live, doesn't she?

What? I'm not picking. I think you and I ought to have a heart-to-heart talk. . . . About girls, that's what. . . . You what? You're hungry? Waiter! Bring us two large

Cokes until we get ready to order. (*Pause*) How did you come to pick out this place? It's what? Cozy? Like Grand Central Terminal, it's cozy. A violin player comes and fiddles in your soup, I will bet anything.

It's nice of you to squeeze my hand, Shirley. It's very tender. I know there are a lot of things right with girls. It's pretty obvious to any fellow who has good eyesight. But there are a lot of things wrong with them. If these things were corrected the human race would benefit greatly. So would I.

For example: Time. Girls do not understand Time. A minute to you is like a half hour. "I'll be ready in just a minute." How many times have you told me that? I could read all through Dickens while I'm waiting.

If I am supposed to meet you at noon I might as well not show up until one, because you will not show up until two. Why? Because the telephone kept ringing, or your hair wouldn't dry. Why do girls always wash their hair when they have a date?

I know you always apologize, Shirley. You smile and squeeze my hand and *sometimes* I forget you were late. But you were.

Now, Shirley, I am with you like one hundred per cent, but why do girls show up for dates dressed like boys? If a boy dates a girl he wants a *girl* to show up—even if she *is* late. I mean, like those tight slacks, Shirley. Couldn't you take an extra ten minutes and put on a dress? What? . . . This isn't formal? Shirley, just because something is not formal does not mean you can show up with a sweater with M.I.T. across it.

No, I'm not just mad because you were late. You are always late. But this stuff has been bursting inside me. I love you, Shirley, but do you have to get a haircut like the Yale crew? And, Shirley, I am six feet six inches tall. You do not have to wear loafers to make me feel superior.

I what, Shirley? I feel superior, anyway? No, Shirley, I am just curious. If we are going steady and going to spend our lives together after I get through college and pre-med and medical and post-medical and internship and all—we ought to know how we stand.

If you dress that way to show you don't care, why do you show up at all? . . . You what? You feel comfortable in those clothes? I've seen you when your pants and sweater were so tight you had to stand up all evening, and you say you're more comfortable that way!

All right. Forget the clothes. Take the telephone. I called three times and the line was busy. That's why a woman's work is never done, as the poet says, because she's on the telephone. A girl's telephone is always busy. I know a very rich girl, Shirley, and she has *three* telephones and they're always busy. She talks out of both sides of her mouth, I guess, and plays phonograph records in the middle. What, Shirley? It's a joke. See . . . with three telephones . . . never mind, Shirley. It's nothing to joke about.

What do girls *do* on the telephone, Shirley? They're supposed to be eagerly awaiting calls from their boy friends, but how can they get calls when they're tying up the line? I'll bet thousands of girls would be engaged right now, or be pinned, or be out eating grinders, if anybody could reach them.

I suspect, Shirley, that you use the telephone to play both sides of a Modern Jazz Quartet album for your friends over the phone. Or you are running down somebody. Why do girls always run down people, Shirley? You don't? All right. What do you think of Mazie Donahue? Isn't she pretty? . . . Oh? She's beautiful if I like that cheap, obvious kind of beauty? See? What about Betty Wendell? Popular as anything. What about her? Huh? Who wants to be popular that way? Is that what you said?

O.K. Another thing, Shirley. You get three or four girls together, and all you hear is whispers, giggles, double-talk and deep sighs. And what do these girls talk about when they do speak a few understandable words? They do not talk about sane, important things like football, fishing, hunting, hockey, Bardot and sports cars. They talk about two things: clothes and boys. Mostly they talk about clothes.

All these things confuse me, Shirley. When we are married and I am the leader and strong-minded head of the house, just for an example—I know it's years away—are you going to go on being like this, Shirley? (*Pause*) Don't look at the menu yet, dear. Just let me finish. Just give me an answer. . . . What? You're a woman? You're *supposed* to be flighty and fickle and moody and late? You're *feminine?*

I knew it. Always an excuse and the same excuse. Look, Shirley dear, I'm crazy about you. But I wish you would try and be a little more like me—level-headed, clear-eyed, calm, punctual and frugal.

Frugal. Yes.

What, Shirley? Then you wouldn't be feminine? Can't you be feminine in matters that . . . that. . . . You don't have to be nutty to be feminine. . . . What? It helps?

Oh, you're hungry, dear. O.K. Look at the menu. Just

keep in mind I'm trying to smooth out our future together, see? It's pure unselfishness. Now, look, Shirley, before you order, I have one favor to ask. I know you're starved. That's why I ask it. It so happens I'm a little short this week. Broke would be a more accurate word. I was wondering if you had ten bucks mad money you could let me have. (*Pause*)

I knew you would, Shirley. You're really an angel. Thanks. Why not have the lobster stuffed with lobster? It's only $4.50.

THE END

25 | KNOTS

(*This act may be done by a man or woman. It may be performed with or without an actual piece of rope. The performer should chuckle apologetically when something does not quite come off.*)

Good evening, ladies and gentlemen, and welcome to a few minutes of knots. Knots to you, I call this little demonstration. With a simple piece of rope some of the most amazing knots in the world can be made.

By the way, this piece of rope happens to be the piece with which Napoleon was hanged. I know Napoleon wasn't hanged but if he had been this piece of rope would have done it (*Pause*) easily. It has historic value, you see.

Now this is a simple bow—the sort you use on shoes or Christmas packages. (*Takes rope and twists it around into a silly knot. Holds it up*) This isn't exactly what I meant, but it will give you an idea. This actually is a surgeon's reef knot or a round-turn and one-half hitch. I'm not sure which. This end looks like a half hitch. (*He unties it.*)

The history of knots is very interesting. Primitive man

did not know about knots. He just kept wrapping rope around something. The Egyptians knew about knots but they kept most of it a secret. From me, anyway. (*He is tying some kind of complicated knot while he talks, grunting now and then.*) It was not until the Middle Ages that knots were discovered, when Sir Wilfred Knott was idling away an afternoon in his falconry, and picked up a piece of rope and tied it in a knot. "Eureka!" he cried, thinking he had really discovered something.

He showed it to Lady Knott, and she just shrugged. Sir Wilfred was so disappointed that he tied about forty knots that day and had them roasted for dinner. (*Pause*) Tough, too. He used an inferior grade of rope and no tenderizer.

(*Lifts up the rope and shows a weird bunch of twists.*) The double—it might even be triple—wine-keg knot, used all over France to lift wine kegs into drinking position. Notice this end of the rope sinks to permit the keg to be raised to the mouth. Functional. (*Unties the knot and starts another*)

My next knot will be a standing-sitting double twist with a granny hitch followed by two figure eights. This has never been done before. (*He works away carefully at the knot.*)

This knot is useless. (*Pause*) There are peculiar circumstances surrounding it. It is the only knot that can be safely used to tie up a hummingbird safely. On the other hand, it cannot be tied with anything but a rope so large that the hummingbird just walks right out of it. The Greeks called this a paradox. A paradox is a statement that contradicts itself. Like, "This pig doesn't weigh as much as I expected, but I didn't think it would."

I like to keep you entertained with these little items while

I'm doing the knots, because sometimes they take hours. (*Lifts up rope bunched confusedly into a heap*) There we are! (*Looks at it, puzzled*) Actually, this is *not* the knot I started to do. I'm so creative. This is a triple clove hitch surrounded by two reef knots and a knee-bend. I imagine it would look nice framed in natural walnut.

And now, ladies and gentlemen, the most valuable knot of all—a knot that cannot become loosened, a knot that gets tighter every time you try to loosen it—a really permanent knot for many situations. But first I'll show you a temporary version. (*He puts the rope around his neck and ties a four-in-hand necktie knot. As he talks he draws the knot tighter and tighter around his neck.*) If you ever want to tie up a criminal so he cannot possibly escape (*Chokes slightly, then goes on*) this . . . knot (*Coughs*) is . . . recommended. (*It is more and more difficult for him to talk.*)

How strange. I believe I've tied the permanent knot after all. (*Coughs again. Pulls on knot and throws his head back*) You will notice . . . that any attempt I make—like this—to loosen the knot (*Gasps*) only . . . (*Coughs*) makes it (*Gives a squeaking noise*) worse, and. . . . Help! Help! I'm choking! Help! (*He rushes offstage gasping.*)

THE END

26 | YOUR MONEY CHEERFULLY REFUNDED

(This is for a woman. She is MRS. EVERWRAUGHT, *who has taken seriously all the assurances sales clerks have given her in times past that "if it's the wrong size, it can be easily exchanged or your money refunded." She suggests with her pantomiming that she is carrying an atomizer.* MRS. EVERWRAUGHT *should begin at one end of the stage and move across gradually, to indicate going from one section of a store to the other.)*

Young lady. Young lady! Yes, I know, but I've been standing here for ten minutes—right in this very spot at the perfume counter. . . . Well, I'm sure *you've* been standing here all day too, but that is your job. (*Nervous pause.* MRS. EVERWRAUGHT *pretends to pick up one thing or another but without any real interest.*) Young *lady*. Oh. Are you the young lady who . . . was the young lady . . . I don't have my glasses . . . well, at any rate, my husband gave me this perfume for my birthday. I wanted a mink stole, but that's another story. Not a very entertaining one, either. Well, when I opened the package, imagine my surprise when I found it was Fatal Swoon. My husband was

never very good at scents. What? My dear young lady, I
have worn Lazy Geranium for years. I just put on a little
extra when I'm going out. When people smell Lazy Geranium, they know it's *me*. What do I want? My dear
young lady, I saw the most attractive drip-dry nylon and
cotton blouse across the street at Waterbury & Krunch and
—I beg your pardon? You have to wait on this gentleman?
He's been waiting a long time? Young lady, I do not see
how he could have been waiting when he just arrived
. . . young—! (*She stops wearily, turns away and mumbles
as if talking to herself.*)

I never knew it to fail. You can have a hundred women
mobbed before a counter and let a *man* appear—almost
any man—and the salesgirl will simply ignore everyone
else. I should have sent Harvey to exchange this himself,
but he said he had blushed and fussed and been nervous
ENOUGH buying it in the first place, trapped, as he put
it, between Desperation Number Three and Midnight
Steam.

(*Turns back to counter*) Miss . . . Miss . . . You were
waiting on me. Yes. What did I want? My dear girl, I'm
getting exhausted. I didn't have my second cup of coffee
today, and it does things to me. This perfume in this
package is too exotic. It is also too heavy. Men are romantic. They are always buying exotic things. Either they are
romantic or they are not paying attention. Smell it! (*She
squirts atomizer.*) No one should ever sell any of this melo-
dramatic stuff to MEN. They don't use it themselves. They
use Scorched Leather or Corona Corona Number Nine.

I am sure you are busy. I am busy, too. I'm chairman of
the Blue Feather Fund, vice-president of the Canasta Club
and the mother of two irritating children. I love them, of

course, but they can be a trial. . . . I *told* you what I wanted. I want my money back. I am CERTAIN this over-powering scented ether set my husband back a pretty penny. . . . You are not empowered to give refunds? Will I please take something else in exchange? I will not. I want my money back. There are signs all over the place to the effect that if I am not satisfied—and I am *not* satisfied—my money will be cheerfully refunded, no questions asked and no red tape, either. Now . . .

Who? The floor manager. Is that he beside the elevator? Oh, that's a dummy displaying men's swim trunks. I did think he looked a bit underdressed for the job. My glasses, you know. And that certainly is not a natural tan.

Where? Oh, I see. Well, I don't see why I have to run all over Bronson and Reed's department store for a simple thing like this. . . . Oh, I know, you are well-trained, you girls—like the secret service. Make it hard for the customer and she'll give up. Well, I won't. Bronson and Reed shall know I have been here.

(*She takes her package with a sigh and walks away, looking about. Finally she stops.*) Young man. Young man! You *are* the floor manager? I can tell by the carnation. My name is Everwraught. Of the Suffield Everwraughts. . . . Yes. We were here before the Cabots. We greeted them. And the Lodges, too. And you are? . . . Mr. Duffle. Mr. Duffle, I shall not detain you long from your pilgrimages up and down the aisles. The matter is simple. I have here heaven knows how many ounces of the alleged perfume, Fatal Swoon. I'm Lazy Geranium, myself. No, I do not want any more Lazy Geranium. At the moment I have plenty of Lazy Geranium. What? What's wrong with Fatal Swoon? Smell it! (*Sprays*) You see! You had to duck. . . .

Beg pardon? No, I have *not* used any of it. I couldn't. It goes against my grain. Bardot, perhaps. Sophia Loren, maybe. But definitely not me. I have enough trouble. Using this could get me evicted from the P. T. A. Here, take it, Mr. Duffle. (*Holds it out*)

Mr. Duffle, *please* do not squirt it at ME. Well, *you* might like it . . . possibly for cleaning your typewriter or getting spots off your necktie or chewing gum off your shoes. What? I am NOT losing my temper. I lost it long ago.

What I want, Mr. Duffle, is my money back. . . . You what? You are not empowered to give refunds? Mr. Duffle, it says very clearly all over the place that my money will be cheerfully . . . What? . . . Oh, when I do get it, I will get it cheerfully. Speak to whom? The complaint manager? Down the corridor. How can I be sure it doesn't contain a trap door that will spring and send me down into the basement where I shall be placed on a rack and . . . Well, I wouldn't be surprised at anything. What are you HERE for if not to refund money? (*Pause*) You've never really found out, yourself? Well, that makes it cozy. Mr. Duffle, believe me, no matter how you try to wear me down I shall not give up. I shall get my money back from Bronson and Reed's department store and torture chamber. The name of Mrs. Everwraught will cause cold shudders to go up and down the spines of both Bronson and Reed. I shall not give up, Mr. Duffle. Let me have the perfume. (*Takes it*)

(*She turns away and walks a bit, looking about. Then she pretends to open a door, stops, and waits.*) Mr. Gilli water? I *did* knock. How was *I* to know you were practicing putting? You are the complaint manager, are you not?

You look as if you should be. You have that dour, sour, long, mournful face. Pardon me? . . . Yes, it is obvious I am not here to exchange compliments. I will be brief, Mr. Gilliwater, since I have now reached the heights. I have here a quart or so of Fatal Swoon perfume that my husband bought for me. It is too heavy and not ME. Smell! (*Squirts*)

I simply wish my money back. . . . No, I do not have the receipt. Husbands do not save sales slips. You certainly may examine the bottle. Squirt it all over. I bet it will kill flies. But enough of this, Mr. Gilliwater. Bronson and Reed guarantee . . . Bronson and Reed . . . Bronson. . . . It what? It does not come from Bronson and Reed's? It was in a Bronson and Reed box. . . . What? The perfume plainly says, "Bottled exclusively in Hong Kong for Carter and Wallingford? Where? Inside the bottle? Well, that's a fine place to put it. (*Pause*) Hong Kong! French perfume?

Now I have to go all the way to the other end of town to Carter and Wallingford's and go through the same torment again. (*Pause*) Your wife does what? Bathes in Fatal Swoon? Just the thing, Mr. Gilliwater. Shall we say twenty dollars, Mr. Gilliwater? Fifteen? Ten? Done, Mr. Gilliwater. I'm sure your wife will be delighted with it. There is nothing that sets a woman up more, I always say, than a present from her husband of something mysterious and romantic. Yes. Ten dollars. Thank you.

And if she doesn't like it, Mr. Gilliwater, just let me know. Just simply ask for your money back. (*Pauses triumphantly*) And see if you get it! (*Turns and stalks out*)

THE END

27 | WRITE A JINGLE

(The president of the Gookie Soap Company is sitting behind his desk. He speaks to an imaginary group of employees before him.)

Gentlemen, we have received an overwhelming response to the Gookie Soap Jingle contest. In fact, we have so many entries, as you can see from the mountainous piles about my desk, that I have decided to pick the winner myself. We have five minutes before the deadline when we announce to the press and an eager world the winners in our sensational contest.

Now, you fellows understand why I waited till the last minute, I guess. I wanted to give every soap-loving American a fair and square chance to send in that wrapper or box top. Soap is the backbone of America. A clean America is a strong America. Our nation has always been and will always be tops in the soap race.

And it's no secret to you men, from first vice-presidents down to fourth vice-presidents, that when it comes to good living, when it comes to togetherness, statistics prove the family that uses Gookie soap is the family that stays together.

Now, fellows, we want to be fair about this contest. We don't want to give away valuable prizes to people just because they are eggheads and can write good poetry. Nor do we want to honor smart alecks who happen to be smarter than we normal people. So I am going to judge this contest by instinct.

Harry, you're the ranking vice-president. Please step up here and blindfold me, and I will judge the quality of these jingles by picking the winners out of the pile. (*Pretends he is being blindfolded*) All right, Harry, not too tight now. Oh, that's not quite tight enough. (*Pretends to peer over blindfold*) I can still see a little. Let's make sure this is fair and square. . . . All right, now turn me around a few times, Harry. (*Spins around, becomes dizzy, staggers*) There. That's just right. O.K. First I will draw for fifth prize, a gold-plated moose call for a man, or a rubber rolling pin for a woman.

(*He reaches into pile and selects a slip. He pretends to lift blindfold and reads.*)

Gookie soap gives you hope
When your stuff is dirty:
Overalls or coveralls,
Lingerie or shirtee.

Isn't that touching? Mrs. George Minx of Boise, Idaho. Notice how she gets in all those sentimental garments? Good for Mrs. Minx.

All right. Back with the blindfold. (*Covers eyes again*) There we are. For fourth prize, a life-size statue of our founder, Fred J. Gookie, carved in soap. (*Reaches into pile selects a slip. Takes off blindfold and reads.*) Oh, fellows, this *is* beautiful. It's from Mrs. Freeda Whipple of Selma, Alabama. (*He recites this one touchingly.*)

Sunset and evening star
And one clear soap for me.
And let there be no soap but Gookie soap
With Monday's wash for me.

Doesn't that get you *here?* (*Touches his heart*) I mean, it's truly a beautiful sentiment, and so original. I can almost see, through the mist of soapsuds, the clean, smiling faces of these people who love our soap so much.

Well, let's get on, fellows. I don't want to start weeping. The blindfold again, and we're ready for third prize, an all-expense two-week vacation on an isolated island off the coast of Greenland. Let's see, now. (*He moves his hands around and picks out another winner. Removes blindfold and reads*)

Hail to thee, blithe Gookie!
Bird thou never wert.
But what's the blasted difference?
You sure get rid of dirt.

Say! That's real *poetry.* "Hail to thee, blithe Gookie!" Isn't that lovely? Shelley couldn't have done better. I tell you, fellows, this is a deep emotional experience. I mean, when I think of how our soap stirs the hearts of the people, I could almost *give* it away. (*Pause*) Ha ha. Well, not quite. Anything you get for nothing you don't appreciate. (*Looks at paper*) That was from Mrs. Albert Fiddelback of Cranberry, Massachusetts. We're proud to have her in the Gookie family.

And now for second prize, a seventy-five year supply of Gookie detergent, a new Rolls Royce and a complete college education at the University of California, or its equivalent in frozen foods. (*Picks up another slip and reads it to himself.*)

Gentlemen, I don't see how they can get much better. This one . . . well, I am stirred. It's *glorious*. It marches! It has a swing to it. Listen to this. It's from Mrs. Jeanne d'Arc O'Brien of Big Squirt, Texas.

> Allons enfants de la patrie!
> Gookie soap is la soap for me!
> Le jour de gloire est arrivé.
> It washes clothes as bright as day!

I'll bet you don't get this sort of stuff in other jingle contests. This proves what I always have said: That Gookie soap users are a race apart in loyalty, cleanliness and heart.

Now, gentlemen, we have reached an historic peak. We are ready for the first prize, an annual income of $7,000 a year for life, hospitalization insurance, your own eight-hole golf course, a trip to Tanzania with one wife, one child and one mother-in-law, all expenses paid, including a hunting safari, plus a mink coat, twenty tons of Gookie soap, a herd of purebred Jersey cows and a fifty-foot yacht. (*Puts on blindfold and picks a slip*)

All right now, hold your breaths. Here it is! The first-prize winner. This goes to lucky, lucky Mrs. Elvis Fabian of Ho-Ho-Kus, New Jersey. Oh, fellows, this is a master-piece. Never in my life have I read anything that glows like this . . . *glows* with life and truth and beauty. (*He recites this with great feeling.*)

Well, I never had clothes so bright before.
Hey, houn' dog, yappy poo pug dope.
Hey, rock around the block, dear.
Hey, give the door a knock, dear.
Hey, houn' dog, Gookie's great soap!
Well, hey! Slap my wrist.
Said, hey! Do the Twist!
Well, hey! Knock my block around the clock.
Stamp, stomp, stamp stomp, willy-nilly,
Stamp and shout, you're no dope!
Dig that way-out
Gets the gray out,
Low down, crazy
Gookie soap.

Man, I tell you that's really with it! The great contest
is over. As a salute to our magnificent winners I'm going
to sing the last few lines of our prize-winner. (*Pretends to
pick up guitar and strum it as he sings.*)

Stamp, stomp, stamp stomp, willy-nilly,
Stamp and shout, you're no dope!
Dig that way-out
Gets the gray out,
Low down, crazy
Gookie soap.

THE END

28 | THE POET SPEAKS

(THE MASTER OF CEREMONIES *comes onstage and addresses the audience.*)

It is an honor to present the poet Reginald Capithorne, who will recite a few of his own modern verses—so don't expect them to make too much sense in the old-fashioned Tennyson and Longfellow way. I want to say about Mr. Capithorne that he came into this world a helpless infant and, using barely more than his two hands, has worked his way to his present age. He has been awarded a number of trophies and so on. At the Van Pierce Junior High last year, as he recited several of his poems, his admirers presented him with tomatoes, small cabbages, old potatoes and other vegetables. Usually Mr. Capithorne recites behind a net, but tonight we feel certain you will all appreciate him. So, here he is, Reginald Capithorne, reciting his own poems.

(THE MASTER OF CEREMONIES *exits. Offstage, he quickly changes his jacket, puts on a flowing tie and a wig, and re-enters as the poet* REGINALD CAPITHORNE. *He is nervous, and full of wild gestures, which often do not illustrate his*

*point at all. He carries a sheaf of manuscript pages. He
bows, as if to the* M.C.)

Thank you for your unnecessary comments. I have recited before the crowned heads of Europe, the bald heads
of New York, and now the swelled heads of Hazardsville.
As a nation we spend ten times as much money on lipsticks
as we spend on poetry. We spend fifty times more on
chickens than we do on poetry. It's true that a poet does
not lay eggs. Usually. But he does have something to con-
tribute to society. I usually read my poems to electric
guitar accompaniment, so you will have to imagine for
yourselves the ceaseless, deafening sound of electric guitars.

For my first poem I have selected a little-known one. It
is called "Red Shoelaces" and is symbolic.

Oh, red shoelaces! (*Throws out one arm*)
Oh, red, *red* shoelaces! (*Throws out both arms*)
Where are you now,
Anyhow? (*Lowers his head in sorrow*)
Together we played many a basketball game as was a
    squeaker,
While you, red shoelaces, faithfully held together a
    sneaker.
Ah, yesteryear. Ah, cold root beer!
Boiled red shoelaces, anguishing in a lamb stew!
Out of place. Lost! Cooked until turning blue!
Oh, red shoelaces!
Oh, red, *red* shoelaces!
How did you get out of my scrapbook into the pot?
Destined for a gourmet's dinner you were definitely
    not. (*Beats his breast with anguish*)
Ah, when will they ever learn, the gods of fate!
That youth is fleeting and red shoelaces do not end

on a plate,
Garnished with yesterday's dreams,
As out of the stewpot steams
Red, red, red shoelaces, *red, red* shoelaces,
Leading me on and on to *new, new* faces.

Gesundheit!
(*He bows, fumbles, and drops the manuscript of the poem on the floor.*)
Don't applaud until the end, please. It breaks the mood. Now I have something more cheerful. It is very short, I mean. It is simple but provoking. It is called, "Escape from Early Death and a Chance to Sit upside down on the Ceiling Again." (*He pretends, for a moment, to be chasing a fly around the stage, making buzzing sounds, then reads.*)

Oh, little fly is it you again? No, not again.
Miserable, uncultured creature I must swat again!
For you I must make it hot again! (*Swats wildly*)
Go, flee, out the window to land on a garden pot again.
Stay there, with thy thirty-seven blue eyes, lest I swat
    again.

(*He bows and again drops manuscript pages on the floor.*)
No applause, please. Not until the flowers are brought to me at the end. (*Pause*) And now, finally, a love poem I wrote this morning, dedicated to my girl friend, who would like to forget the whole thing. It is called, "I Love You." (*Reads*)

Roses are red
Violets are green.
Sugar is sour,
Vinegar, I mean.

Roses are red,
Teachers are mean,
Apples'll make you
Sick when they're green.

Roses are red,
Peanuts are brown.
If you can't smile
At least you can frown.

Roses are red,
But you're kind of pallid
Yet I love you more
Than a cucumber salad.

I love you more
Than peanuts or honey
'Cause sugar is sweet
And you're kind of funny.

Roses are red
Violets are blue.
I'm not very popular
So you'll have to do.

(*He bows deeply and drops the rest of the manuscript on the floor.*) Applause, now! (*Suddenly looking offstage*) What's that? You have a message for me? From the Mayor? At last! *Recognition!* I'm famous! Give me the message. (*Reaches out as if to take a slip of paper, and pantomimes reading it. Then his face falls.*) It says, "Please do not throw paper on the floor. Put it in the wastebasket!" (*Frantically he gathers up the manuscript pages from the floor and runs out.*)

THE END